To Phil —

Best Wishes

Robert G. Stanger

HOW TO EVALUATE
REAL ESTATE PARTNERSHIPS

ROBERT A. STANGER
with
KEITH D. ALLAIRE

Robert A. Stanger & Co.

Shrewsbury, New Jersey

Other Publications From Robert A. Stanger & Co

Periodicals:

THE STANGER REPORT: A GUIDE TO PARTNERSHIP INVESTING
THE STANGER REGISTER: PARTNERSHIP PROFILES
THE STANGER REVIEW: PARTNERSHIP SALES

Books:

TAX SHELTERS: THE BOTTOM LINE
STANGER'S OIL & GAS PARTNERSHIP PERFORMANCE YEARBOOK
STANGER'S PARTNERSHIP SPONSOR DIRECTORY
HOW TO SELL REAL ESTATE PARTNERSHIPS
THE STANGER REAL ESTATE PARTNERSHIP PERFORMANCE WORKBOOK

Supplements:

FOUR WAYS TO MEASURE INVESTMENT VALUE
REGIONAL DRILLING PROFILES

Published by Robert A. Stanger & Co.
1129 Broad Street, Shrewsbury, New Jersey 07701

Printed in the United States of America.

Library of Congress Catalog Card Number: 85-90539

ISBN 0943570-10-7

ABOUT THE AUTHORS

Robert A. Stanger is recognized as one of the nation's experts on direct investment in oil and gas and real estate. The author of three books in the field, he is frequently quoted in national publications such as *The New York Times, The Wall Street Journal, Barron's, Business Week, Forbes* and *Fortune*.

In 1978 Mr. Stanger founded Robert A. Stanger & Co., publisher of *The Stanger Report: A Guide to Partnership Investing, The Stanger Register: Partnership Profiles,* and *The Stanger Review: Partnership Sales.* The Report, Register and Review have attracted a wide audience of sophisticated readers, primarily accountants, lawyers, financial planners, investment advisors, bankers, brokers and substantial investors.

Before founding the company seven years ago, Mr. Stanger spent 17 years on Wall Street as an investment banker. Most recently, he was vice president and manager of the Tax Incentive Department at Merrill Lynch. Previously, he was first vice president in the Corporate Finance Department of White, Weld & Co.

In these positions, he structured limited partnerships in real estate, oil and gas, and such other areas as cattle, cable television, and equipment leasing. He also originated and placed mortgage and equity investments in commercial and residential real estate.

A registered investment advisor, he is a member of many professional groups, including the New York Society of Security Analysts, the Oil Investment Institute, the Investment Association of New York, the International Association of Financial Planners, the National Leased Housing Association, the Real Estate Securities and Syndication Institute and the Investment Partnership Association. He is a 1961 graduate of Princeton University, with a bachelor's degree in economics.

Keith D. Allaire began his career with Robert A. Stanger & Co. in 1982 as a financial analyst. Through excellence of research, insight, and ability to direct the efforts of others, Mr. Allaire rose to become head of Stanger's Research and Editorial Department. He directs the activities of investment research and partnership rating personnel, edits *The Stanger Report* and *The Stanger Register* and oversees creation of all books and other publications. Mr. Allaire has had special success in applying analytical techniques to the field of partnership investing.

Mr. Allaire graduated from Trinity College in 1969 with a degree in Mathematics, then attended Cornell University's Graduate School of Business and Public Administration. His academic achievements earned him an RCA Science Scholarship, a James Lippincott Goodwin Fellowship and a Cornell University Graduate Fellowship. After pursuing a career in professional music, he completed his M.B.A. in Finance at Fairleigh Dickinson University. Mr. Allaire is Mr. Stanger's editor, sounding board, principal contributor and is responsible for the formulation and execution of this book.

ACKNOWLEDGMENTS

This book reflects the on-going commitment of Robert A. Stanger & Co. to foster uniform standards and improve the quality of investment evaluation in the limited partnership industry. We are indebted to the gifted professionals of our Research and Rating Group and our affiliated consulting group, SJW Associates, who have contributed to this effort over many years.

Our special thanks go to Richard Natelson and Kevin Gannon for challenging our ingenuity and helping refine our analytical methods; to Nancy Schabel for her painstaking review and critique of the manuscript; and to Patricia Fogle and Susanne Grajek for their boundless patience and energy in bringing this book to print.

Robert A. Stanger
Keith D. Allaire

CONTENTS

EVALUATION CHECKLISTS AND WORKSHEETS

PREFACE

Real estate partnership investing poses unique challenges to today's sophisticated investors and financial advisors. The investment community acknowledges the potential of real estate partnerships to satisfy a broad range of individual financial objectives and provide superior returns compared with other investment forms. But, matching partnerships with financial goals and picking specific investments which will deliver superior performance is becoming increasingly difficult and time consuming.

In 1985, advisors sifted through more than 2,500 real estate limited partnership ("RELP") offerings and committed in excess of $12 billion of capital for an estimated one million investors. Each investment required a judgment as to the merit of a specific partnership and its suitability for an individual investor.

Beyond sheer numbers, RELPs pose unique challenges due to their relative complexity. RELPs can provide a variety of benefits (tax shelter, current income and capital growth) at different times and in varying proportions. RELPs invest in a broad spectrum of real estate assets with unique risks and returns—office buildings, apartments, shopping centers, condominiums, mini-warehouses, hotels, motels, mobile home parks, land, participating and nonparticipating mortgages, federally insured mortgages, etc.

Unlike typical stock, bond or mutual fund investments, each partnership is a uniquely structured agreement between investors (limited partners) and the manager of the business (general partner). The investor's share of profits is defined by complex terms and conditions which are often difficult to analyze. Advisors need to assess not only the economic outlook for the industry and management's skill (as with stocks and bonds), but also the impact of profit-sharing arrangements within the partnership.

Assessing management skill is more difficult for partnerships than for corporate investments. Required financial reporting is on a "historic cost" basis which does not reflect the market value of the partnership's assets. Even where information is provided, meaningful industry-wide standards do not exist, making valid comparisons almost impossible. Learning how management has performed in prior partnerships is often a herculean undertaking, requiring the advisor to interpret and standardize dissimilar data.

The dynamic environment and dramatic growth of partnership investing also places huge demands on investors and advisors. New types of RELP investments are constantly being created. Regulatory rules and tax laws change continuously. How do you make sure today's "good" investment won't be tomorrow's disaster?

How to Evaluate Real Estate Partnerships is designed to help investment professionals and professional investors overcome these challenges. This book is the product of six years of work by the Partnership Research Group of Robert A. Stanger & Co.— work developing analytical techniques, quantitative methods, and objective measures of comparison which are now recognized as standards throughout the industry.

Whether you are a financial planner, stockbroker, CPA, tax specialist or a sophisticated investor, *How To Evaluate Real Estate Partnerships* gives you state-of-the-art tools and techniques to save time and make superior investment decisions.

The book provides "high-powered" evaluation techniques for professionals experienced in the analysis of limited partnership investments. Sections II through IV present step-by-step procedures and techniques for in-depth evaluation of public programs, private placements and sponsor organizations. Section V provides a unique method for assessing the progress of existing partnership investments.

At the same time, we've tried to create a bridge for less experienced pros who want to develop specialized skill in the partnership investment area. An introductory section explains the unique attributes and benefits of real estate and the partnership vehicle. Section I provides a step-by-step technique for matching real estate partnership investments with individual financial goals and risk tolerance and presents a closer look at alternative types of RELPs.

INTRODUCTION

WHY INVEST IN REAL ESTATE?

CHAPTER 1

REAL ESTATE:
THE PREDICTABLE INVESTMENT

Real estate investment is an appealing way to make money grow. Prices are not volatile and investment results are attractive relative to stocks and bonds. The reasons: demand (demographics), the construction/lending cycle, the independence of markets for different types of property and the opportunistic nature of real estate investors.

For investors with the time, the aptitude and the cash to change occupations or take on a new profession on a moonlighting basis, do-it-yourself real estate investing offers attractive rewards. Anything from renting out a single-family house to developing office buildings and shopping centers is possible and many first-time investors/developers have succeeded.

More likely, the best way for an investor to benefit from powerful real estate economics is through real estate limited partnerships ("RELPs"). A RELP is like a mutual fund. Investors contribute capital and a real estate professional or organization (the general partner) constructs and manages a portfolio of income-producing properties. RELPs allow investors to take advantage of the many factors making real estate a predictable and productive investment.

ECONOMIC FACTORS

Real estate investment opportunities are created by construction cycles (which influence supply) and the reliable long-term growth of households, population and employment (demand). Lending and construction cycles drive real estate prices. When lenders lend, builders build. When a type of property in a particular location is in short supply, rent levels and return on investment are rising. Eventually, lenders make construction funds available for developers. Buildings pop up. As the supply of space increases, competition brings rents down. When return on investment falls, lenders reduce the flow of financing and new construction slows. Time allows demand from demographics to catch up, and the cycle starts over.

In a climate of mild or increasing inflation, buildings cost more to build in the future. So even if overbuilding occurs in the short run, higher costs of new construction will make the older building a bargain eventually.

When new building slows, demand tends to catch up to the available space. As population, employment and the number of households grow, demand increases for apartments, office buildings and shopping centers. Over 15 million new households will be formed during the 1980s, and white collar employment will grow by over 26%.

Increased demand for real estate translates into higher rent. Rising rents lead to appreciation of property values and generate investment opportunities. Overall, rents rose an average of 5% per annum from 1964 to 1984 and even faster from 1980 to 1984.

In addition to demographics, investment demand for U.S. real estate is growing. Pension funds, which now hold $30 billion in real estate assets, are expected to expand their holdings to $200 billion by 1990, dramatically increasing demand for investment-grade properties. By world standards, U.S. real estate is bargain priced. So, stimulated foreign investment should also help increase property values.

INDEPENDENCE OF MARKETS

Price cycles for different types of property usually do not coincide. Factors causing demand for apartments in a particular location may not be applicable to office buildings in another location. A few years ago, demand for large enclosed mall shopping centers was widespread, pushing prices to relatively high levels, while office building prices declined due to overbuilding.

Property price cycles also vary significantly by location. Urban and suburban office markets have unique characteristics. Prices in the Sunbelt are driven by entirely different factors than in the Northeast. The demographics in Florida, Michigan and Oklahoma are not the same.

The result is that investment opportunities are always present in real estate. Sophisticated, knowledgeable investors can generate opportunities to buy and sell. Judging relative values enables investors to take advantage of imperfect local property markets. Skillful real estate entrepreneurs and investment managers can produce superior performance. But, doing better than the market is only a bonus added to the inherent benefits of real estate.

REAL ESTATE INVESTMENT PERFORMANCE

Investment performance of income-producing real estate in general has been outstanding. The pretax average annual return from 1951 to 1978 was 13.9% according to a 28-year study of statistical data collected by the American Council of Life Insurance. Nominal pretax returns (not adjusted for inflation) varied from a respectable 11.7% during the low inflationary period of 1951–1968 to 18.0% during the high inflationary period of 1969–1978. The inflation-adjusted return stayed fairly constant at 10.3% annually.

From 1970 to 1984, real estate clearly outperformed other investments. Average quarterly inflation-adjusted returns of the

Prudential Property Investment Separate Account, one of the largest U.S. real estate investors, exceeded returns on money market instruments, long-term bonds and common stocks, according to the research of Goldman Sachs & Co. During the period 1971 to 1984, according to a study published by Liquidity Fund Investment Corporation, sixty-six appreciation-oriented real estate limited partnerships returned 13.2% annually after tax to a 38% tax bracket investor. This return far surpassed compound annual after-tax returns of 4.9% on Treasury Bills, 6.7% for The New York Stock Exchange Composite Index and 2.3% for long-term corporate bonds.

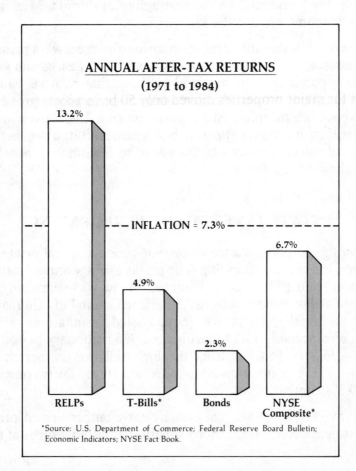

ANNUAL AFTER-TAX RETURNS
(1971 to 1984)

13.2%

---- INFLATION = 7.3% ----

6.7%

4.9%

2.3%

RELPs   T-Bills*   Bonds   NYSE Composite*

*Source: U.S. Department of Commerce; Federal Reserve Board Bulletin; Economic Indicators; NYSE Fact Book.

STABLE PRICING

Prices of properties, measured by capitalization rates (yields buyers require), remain relatively stable over business cycles and have remained relatively stable over the years. Over the last twenty years, capitalization rates for net operating income (rents less operating expenses before debt service) have ranged from 8% to 10%. Most stock traders and fixed income investors would be ecstatic if financial markets fluctuated so narrowly.

Putting real estate prices in stock market terms, price/earnings ratios for real estate have ranged from 10 to 12 since the early 1960s. During the same period, the price/earnings ratio of the Dow Jones Average ranged from 6 to 21.

Here's another example. In a three-month period recently, long-term interest rates increased about 200 basis points (two percentage points). At the same time, real estate capitalization rates for major properties moved only 50 basis points (one-half of one percentage point).

In commercial real estate, the earnings stream is protected somewhat by long-term leases. So, upswings and downswings in rents are mitigated. The relative stability of income (earnings) is one reason the range in valuation is much less for real estate than for other financial instruments.

Another reason capitalization rates for real estate are within narrow limits is the relationship between the real estate income stream and inflation. Yields increase to offset inflation because rents go up. So, the current yield does not need to reflect inflation expectations, only a return for the use of money. Bond yields must reflect both, so fluctuations in bond yields are greater in a volatile economy.

For example, suppose real estate yields are 9% and bond yields are 12%. If long-term interest rates rise to 14%, current yields on real estate will not go up the full 2%. Why? Buyers will expect property income to rise over time to give them a higher yield eventually.

Even the impact of long-term mortgage rates on real estate prices is less than you might expect. The reason: Interest rates reflect the expected rate of inflation. In general, if interest rates are high, so are inflation expectations. Even if mortgage interest and principal repayment take more of the net operating income, leveraged earnings will increase faster as inflation pushes up rents. So, property prices expressed in terms of a multiple of net operating income (which pays both debt service and earnings on equity investment) may not change much.

For example, suppose mortgage loans cost 10%, and you are willing to buy property with an 8% yield on the equity, or cash, portion of the purchase price. If mortgage rates increase to 12% because of inflation, you may be willing to make only 4% currently on your equity investment. You will be confident inflation will increase your cash return rapidly. Under either interest cost scenario, the total property price would be similar.

OUTLOOK

Real estate will continue to create attractive investment results. However, success will depend on shrewd property acquisitions and management to increase value. Real estate investment in the 1980s will not benefit from the inflation-induced appreciation which created superior results in the 1970s. Selectivity is now crucial. Likewise, to take advantage of independent regional cycles, investors must have both knowledge and ability to acquire a variety of property types in several markets. The typical investor lacks this expertise.

Limited partnerships, with their diversification and professional management, allow investors to capitalize on the strengths of today's real estate market. Partnerships have helped millions of investors make real estate investing not only profitable but also relatively predictable.

CHAPTER 2

THE KEY BENEFITS OF
REAL ESTATE PARTNERSHIPS

For most investors, real estate limited partnerships are the best way to take advantage of real estate's powerful economics. By selecting the right real estate limited partnership investment, investors gain easy access to today's broad and diverse real estate market.

In a limited partnership, the investor contributes capital and assumes limited liability. The sponsor, or general partner, manages the affairs and investment activities of the partnership and assumes unlimited liability for partnership debts. The general partner provides the many skills and resources required for successful real estate investing. Pooling your investment with others enables you to buy first-class, larger properties and provides potential diversification.

Investment partnerships come in two varieties: "private" and "public." Private partnerships are exempt from registration with the Securities and Exchange Commission ("SEC"). Typically, they are offered to a small group of investors, require substantial investment (usually over $40,000) and often purchase only one property. In contrast, public partnerships are registered with the SEC and are offered to a large group of investors. They require a relatively modest minimum investment (as low as $2,000) and generally invest in a diversified portfolio of properties.

Public RELPs are the mutual funds of real estate investment. Most individuals lack sufficient capital to diversify their real estate investments. By investing in a public RELP with many other individuals, investors achieve diversification in terms of both geography and property type. Risk of adverse local conditions or cyclical swings in one type of real estate is reduced.

Diversification often translates into staying power—a key attribute of successful real estate investing. In a broad-based portfolio, properties with healthy cash flow can help temporarily beleaguered properties weather the storm. This is particularly important with leveraged real estate because a supplementary source of cash flow can spell the difference between keeping the property and foreclosure.

RELPs, both public and private, can also put investors in the big leagues when it comes to property quality. High-grade office buildings cost upwards of $100 million, beyond the reach of individual investors unless they band together in a partnership.

Finally, RELPs provide some of the best and most knowledgeable management talent available. Remember, real estate is not a passive investment like securities. Each property in the partnership portfolio is a separate business requiring day-to-day management. Decisions must be made and paperwork maintained. Limited partners need experienced management to maximize the potential value and return from properties.

Top management talent also provides financial sophistication—a must in today's real estate markets. Getting the best buy requires knowledge of mortgage markets and financing techniques. The lowest price often goes to those who can structure the deal to solve the seller's tax and financial objectives.

GETTING THE RIGHT BENEFITS

Today's partnerships offer investors as many choices as a well-stocked shoe store. Each property type offers a unique combination of risk and return. And, specific financial benefits (for example, tax benefits versus current cash flow or capital growth) vary depending on the type of partnership selected. The challenge is to find a "comfortable fit"—a partnership suitable for the investor's objectives and risk constraints. Securities regulators have an interest in making sure this happens, but prudent investors must go far beyond the regulatory standards. A method for establishing true "suitability" and selecting the appropriate investment is covered in Section I.

SECTION I

SELECTING A REAL ESTATE PARTNERSHIP INVESTMENT

CHAPTER 3

MATCHING INVESTORS AND INVESTMENTS: A FOUR-STEP PLAN

What makes an investor "suitable" for a real estate limited partnership? According to the SEC, the critical criteria are the investor's annual income and net worth (exclusive of home, furnishings and automobile). For instance, according to a regulatory standard for most public leveraged real estate partnerships, the investor must have either (1) net worth of $100,000, exclusive of personal possessions, or (2) net worth of $50,000 and gross annual income of at least $50,000. (Some states impose higher levels.) For lower-risk income-oriented public RELPs, the investor must have either (1) net worth of $75,000, or (2) net worth of $30,000 and gross annual income of $30,000. In private placements, "accredited" investors must generally have total net worth of $1 million, or gross income of $200,000 for the current year and the previous two years.

But, real estate partnership investors have over 130 public offerings and over 500 private offerings to choose from at any one time. Some sponsors offer five or six different programs. How do you narrow down the field? What's the right investment?

This chapter presents a four-step plan to match investment objectives and RELPs. The orientation is toward public real estate partnerships, but much of the advice applies to suitability for private placements as well. Start by determining investment objectives. Then, assess the risks. Next, match objectives and risk tolerances with types of available public partnerships. Then, see if you are a candidate for a private placement. To simplify the task, many advisors use "Stanger's Guide To Real Estate Partnership Selection" shown on the following page. We suggest you refer to it as you read the rest of this chapter.

STEP 1: DETERMINING YOUR INVESTMENT OBJECTIVES

Investors in a real estate partnership are entitled to know approximately what economic benefits they may receive. The portfolio the sponsor intends to purchase will produce a relatively predictable pattern of taxable income or loss, cash distributions and potential gains. Ask the sponsor what you can expect.

The idea is to match this stream of benefits with your investment objectives. Investors in lower tax brackets might not be able to use tax loss effectively. For tax-exempt accounts, such as IRAs, Keoghs and pension plans, investors might prefer compounding the high current return available in insured mortgage loans. High-bracket investors might prefer limited cash distributions and a real chance at capital growth, available in leveraged partnerships.

You need to consider important personal factors—income, net worth, age, and future income sources and requirements. This introspection helps to quantify acceptable risk and isolate investment objectives. Particular real estate partnerships can accomplish any of the four investment objectives outlined below:

- **Shelter/Growth**—Some public real estate programs offer tax losses to shelter income from other sources. In private programs, the amount of tax savings often equals the capital contributed in initial years. Leverage debt is the important factor in creating this tax loss. The more leverage in a real estate portfolio, the better the opportunity for capital appreciation. Current income is minimal for the first several years of investment in leveraged public programs,

16

STANGER'S GUIDE TO REAL ESTATE PARTNERSHIP SELECTION

Objective	Shelter/Growth	Growth	Growth/Income	Income
Partnership Type	Leveraged	Modestly Leveraged Participating 2nd Mortgage Loans	Unleveraged/ Participating 1st Mortgage Loans	Insured Loans/ Straight-Rate Loans
Maximum Risk	60%–80% Leverage Under Construction Single Property Type Regional 5 Properties or Less	30%–60% Leverage 85%–90% Loan-to-Value Under Construction Single Property Type Regional 5 Properties or Less	0%–30% Leverage 65%–75% Loan-to-Value Under Construction Single Property Type Regional 5 Properties or Less	Non-Insured—90% Loan-to-Value Under Construction Single Property Type Regional 5 Properties or Less
Moderate Risk	60%–80% Leverage Rent-Up Phase Two or more Property Types Limited Geographical Diversification 5 to 15 Properties	30%–60% Leverage 75%–85% Loan-to-Value Rent-Up Phase Two or more Property Types Limited Geographical Diversification 5 to 15 Properties	0%–30% Leverage 65%–75% Loan-to-Value Rent-Up Phase Two or more Property Types Limited Geographical Diversification 5 to 15 Properties	Non-Insured—75% Loan-to-Value Tenanted Two or more Property Types Limited Geographical Diversification 5 to 15 Properties
Lowest Risk	60%–80% Leverage Tenanted Two Property Types or more National 16 Properties or more	30%–60% Leverage 70%–75% Loan-to-Value Tenanted Two Property Types or more National 16 Properties or more	0%–30% Leverage 65%–75% Loan-to-Value Tenanted Two Property Types or more National 16 Properties or more	Insured Loans Tenanted Usually Residential National 16 Properties or more
Tax Status	10%–25% of investment in tax loss during first 12 months	Equities—Tax-free Cash Flow Loans—Taxable	Equities—Partially Tax-free Cash Flow Loans—Taxable	Taxable
Current Yield	5% or Less	Equities—5%–6% Loans—8%–9%	Equities—7%–8% Loans—10%–11%	Loans—11% to 13%

Footnote: Within each risk category, the type of property acquired or loaned against provides a further delineation of risk. The spectrum from most risk to least risk based on property type is: special use facilities and hotels; then apartments and mini-warehouses; then smaller office buildings (less than 250,000 square feet) and community strip shopping centers; then large office buildings and enclosed mall shopping centers; then net leases. For instance, two partnerships could be ranked as Lowest Risk for the objective of Growth. If one purchased hotels and the other office buildings, the former would be more risky than the latter.

usually less than 4%. In private programs you can expect no cash flow during the pay-in period.

- **Growth**—Some partnerships utilize modest leverage (30% to 60% mortgage debt). Here, the appreciation potential is significant but less than when more leverage is employed. Current income is higher than for maximum leverage programs, often starting at 5% to 6% in the first year. Generally speaking, the cash distributions will be tax free (sheltered by depreciation deductions). Some partnerships making participating second mortgage loans are growth investments also—usually with less appreciation potential than modestly leveraged programs but higher current income—typically 8% to 9%. For participating mortgage loan partnerships, all the income is fully taxable (no tax shelter).

- **Growth/Income**—Real estate can be acquired with no mortgage debt, so-called "unleveraged" real estate programs. Growth comes from property economics and not financial leverage. Here, appreciation should equal or exceed the rate of inflation, and current income should be 7% or 8%. Most of the income will be tax sheltered by depreciation. Other qualifying investments for growth/income are more conservative participating first mortgage loan partnerships where current income is around 10% (fully taxable). For this type of mortgage loan partnership and for unleveraged programs, a reasonable level of return is assured, and there are significant opportunities for both growth in income and capital values.

- **Income**—Some partnerships offer portfolios of government insured or non-insured, straight-rate mortgage loans. Competitive levels of current return are available and sometimes current yields are several percentage points above the prime rate, say 11% to 13% today (fully taxable). Modest capital growth, or enhanced return, is possible in some partnerships.

Obviously, investors may buy more than one type of real estate partnership to accomplish multiple investment goals. One partnership might be appropriate for a personal account, while another would be ideal for an IRA or Keogh plan. Participating first and second mortgage loan partnerships are more suitable for lower tax bracket, or tax-free, investors. Unleveraged and leveraged partnerships are more suitable for higher tax bracket investors. Determining up front what you are trying to accomplish with a real estate investment makes the appropriate selection easier later on.

STEP 2: ASSESSING RISK

Suitability requirements don't give you a clue about what risk investors can afford in public partnerships because legal suitability is essentially the same for most public real estate partnerships. (The greater risk of undiversified, highly leveraged private placements is reflected in substantially higher minimum net worth and income requirements.)

However, real estate partnerships, both public and private, can be characterized in terms of risk. You have to look at the kinds of investments the partnership will make. Real estate is like all other investments: The more risk you take, the higher the rate of return you expect to earn. Here are the four risk factors you should consider:

- **Leverage**—The greater the leverage (mortgage borrowing), the greater the risk. Increasing the amount of leverage reduces current cash flow but increases the return from appreciation. The maximum leverage in public real estate partnerships is 80% of property purchase price, but may be set lower. Often the maximum allowable leverage stated in the prospectus is more than the partnership will borrow. Financial advisors should know how much leverage the sponsor intends to use. In private partnerships, leveraging is generally much more aggressive, exceeding 80% of property purchase price. Plus, "staged" private investments (where investors contribute capital over a number of years) even leverage the investors' equity contribution temporarily.

19

For mortgage partnerships, leverage is a risk factor in a different sense. Leverage is measured by the so-called loan-to-value ratio. The more the partnership lends as a percent of what the building is worth, the greater the risk. Loans of 60% to 70% of property value aren't risky. Loans of 80% to 90% of property value are obviously much more risky. Also, some loans are second mortgages or wrap-around mortgages. Here, risk is greater because another lender has a first mortgage, a lien that comes before the partnership in the event of default.

- **The User and the Lease**—Risk in real estate is also a function of the credit of the tenant and the length and terms of the lease. Risk goes from highest to lowest by property type in the following order:

The highest risk is in a special-use property like a fast-food store, because the facility is subject to all the common risks of real estate plus the risk that the special economic use will become unpopular (e.g., too much competition among fast-food stores in the area). Hotels are in the same general high-risk category because they can suffer from wide swings in occupancy. Most hotels depend on over-night rentals, which create the equivalent of a one-day lease. In general, the longer the lease term, the more certain the income stream and the less risky the property.

Apartments and mini-warehouses are rented for longer periods, typically a year or less, and are somewhat less risky. However, they too are subject to swings in occupancy or overbuilding trends.

Office buildings offer risk one step lower because they can reduce risk through a mixture of large and small tenants with lease terms varying from five to ten years. Also, in some cases, tenants bear a portion of operating costs, which reduces risk. (This is not the case in the higher risk categories above. The landlord generally bears all operating costs.) Smaller office buildings may not have the mix of leases and quality tenants which larger buildings enjoy, so their risk is greater.

Shopping centers have longer lease terms and a better tenant mix than most office buildings. Typically, 60% of the space in a center is leased for long periods of time to "credit tenants." Smaller companies fill out the tenant roster, usually with leases of five years or less. Operating expenses usually are passed through to tenants and are not paid by landlords. In terms of risk, large malls and regional shopping centers are less risky than major multi-tenant office complexes; smaller "strip" centers are less risky than smaller office buildings.

The lowest risk category is "net lease" real estate. A building may be rented to a "credit tenant," like General Motors, for a long period of time under what is called a "net lease." Here, the tenant pays all operating and maintenance costs, and also pays the building owner a steady rent check. Not much risk.

- **Construction Phase**—The earlier in the construction process you invest, the more risk you take. Real estate development has three phases. (See the table on the next page.) The first is the building phase—the time before the property is ready for occupancy. Risk potential is in completing the building, incurring building costs which exceed budget, and experiencing construction delays which increase interest carrying costs. The second risk period occurs after completion of construction but before substantial occupancy—the so-called "rent-up" period. Here, owners find out whether they have a good location; whether projected rents are realistic; whether operating costs can be met; and whether cash reserves are sufficient to see the project through to substantial occupancy. The final risk phase is the operational period—the time between completion of rent-up and the ultimate sale of the property. During this period, property owners and managers must negotiate with tenants and determine lease terms and rents; decide on

RISK AND CONSTRUCTION PHASE

Phase	Risk	Risk Elements
Initial Construction	H I G H E R	• Completion problems • Costs in excess of budget • Construction delays • Interest carrying cost
Rent-Up	↑ ⋮ ↓	• Weak location • Operating costs above forecast • Inadequate cash reserves • Soft local market rental conditions
Operation	L O W E R	• Uneconomic lease and rental terms • Repairs and improvements • Management ability • Refinancing or sale decisions

repairs and improvements; maximize returns through effective management; and figure out when to refinance or sell a property. The more of these risks you assume, the higher return you should expect on your investment.

- **Diversification**—Most private real estate partnerships are organized to purchase one property. Some public real estate partnerships are also comparatively small and buy just a few properties. Others raise over $200 million of investor capital and buy up to $500 million of property. In general, the more buildings the partnership owns, the less risk investors are taking. Diversifying geographically spreads the risk of regional economics. Diversifying by property type also reduces risk. In large property pools, investors can own more expensive, higher quality buildings and still achieve diversification.

The four risk factors apply to mortgage debt partnerships as well as equity partnerships because in mortgage deals properties are the collateral. The degree of leverage, the tenant, the timing of the investment or loan in relation to initial construction, and portfolio diversification still determine risk.

You can see that the lowest risk ownership profile would be an unleveraged public partnership with broad diversification in commercial buildings acquired when construction is complete and tenants have moved in. The most risky investment would be a nondiversified, highly leveraged apartment or hotel property private placement in the early stage of development and construction.

STEP 3: UNDERSTANDING INVESTMENT ALTERNATIVES

The threshold choice, public versus private RELP, is usually decided by investor financial suitability requirements and risk tolerance. Although private placements are structured to allow investors to fund contributions largely from tax savings, the size of investment commitments (typically $40,000 or more), the risk of a single property portfolio, and the emphasis on early-year tax shelter makes them appropriate only for high income, high net worth investors.

In contrast, public programs permit relatively small investments ($2,000) and diversify risk. However, risk and investment objectives do vary among public partnerships. Let's look briefly at the five types of public real estate investments typically offered today in terms of investment objective and risk.

- **Leveraged Partnerships**—In leveraged real estate, the cash investment is a downpayment on income-producing properties. The remainder of the purchase price is borrowed from a lending institution and perhaps even from the seller of the property. The investment appeal: Investors have more assets working per dollar of cash, or equity, investment. (See Chapter 5 for a more detailed explanation of leveraged RELPs.)

- Depending on the amount borrowed, leveraged public partnerships are included in either the Shelter/Growth or Growth investment objective category. Even within these categories, risks will vary considerably. Leveraged partnerships can buy properties under construction, which is more risky than buying completed, tenanted buildings. If the leveraged partnership buys apartments, more risk is incurred than with shopping centers. A partnership portfolio consisting of a single property type is more risky than a diversified portfolio.

- **Unleveraged Real Estate**—To keep borrowing costs down, the partnership pays a larger percentage of the property purchase price in cash. Taken to its limit, this technique creates a pure, unleveraged real estate limited partnership. Unleveraged partnerships borrow no money and pay no debt service. The investment appeal: A higher current yield than is available in leveraged programs, less risk, and growth potential for both income and capital. (See Chapter 6 for a more detailed explanation of unleveraged RELPs.)

  Unleveraged partnerships are either in the Growth or Growth/Income category of investment objective. If the partnership buys commercial property, shopping centers or office buildings, growth of principal is relatively assured because of rent escalation clauses in leases. If the partnership buys apartments or hotels, current income should be higher, but obtaining appreciation is less certain because higher rents must be earned in the marketplace. (Real estate risk considerations for unleveraged partnerships are the same as for leveraged partnerships with respect to phase of construction, property type and diversification.) On a comparative basis, unleveraged partnerships provide less appreciation and more current income than leveraged partnerships, but are less risky.

- **Participating Mortgage Loans**—Here, the partnership lends capital in return for interest plus a participation in increases in cash flow and gains from property appreciation. The investment appeal: Interest on a participating mortgage loan is generally higher in the early years than earnings on leveraged or unleveraged partnership investments. (For a more detailed explanation see Chapter 7.)

  Participating first mortgage loan partnerships are in the investment objective category of Growth/Income. The dominant part of the rate of return is the current yield, but the participating feature provides some growth. Participating second mortgage loan partnerships are a little more risky, provide a little less current yield and somewhat greater growth potential. Their investment objective category is Growth. (The degree of risk for both types is determined by the four risk factors outlined earlier.) Comparatively, participating mortgage loan partnerships are much less risky than leveraged equity partnerships and a bit less risky than unleveraged equity partnerships.

- **Insured or Straight-Rate Mortgage Loan Funds**—Insured mortgage partnerships generally buy federally insured mortgages with a lower than current market interest coupon at a discount from principal (par) value. The investment appeal: competitive current yield with enhanced return from early mortgage payoff. There is almost absolute safety of principal when mortgage portfolios are federally insured. Insured loan partnerships are the least risky type of partnership and can provide current yields above yields available in government debt markets.

  Some partnerships make straight-rate mortgage loans either at fixed rates or at rates that fluctuate with the prime rate. Often, these mortgages finance construction and development. Here, the loans can be quite risky, but current return can be above the prime rate.

  Insured or straight-rate mortgage loan partnerships are in the Income category of investment objective. Non-insured, straight-rate loan partnerships run the entire risk spectrum depending on the risk in the real estate they finance. For instance, construction and development loans on apartments are quite risky. Long-term loans on completed, tenanted commercial buildings are comparatively risk free.

- **FREITs**—Finite-life real estate investment trusts ("FREITs") are alternatives to partnerships as vehicles for real estate investing. Cash distributions of a FREIT can be partially tax sheltered by depreciation. FREITs aren't taxed.

Like partnerships, they pass through income directly to investors. FREITs either purchase properties or make mortgage loans and can be leveraged or unleveraged. The primary advantage over partnerships is the liquidity of the shares in the secondary market. The primary disadvantage is that FREITs can't pass through losses, only income. (See Chapter 9 for a detailed description of FREITs.)

FREITs can offer any of the four investment objectives that partnerships offer and any level of risk, depending on the types of investments made. Because a secondary market develops for FREIT shares and not for most partnership interests, FREITs have liquidity and are less risky than partnerships. FREITs should be compared with each other in terms of investment objective and risk by the same method outlined above for partnerships.

Chapters 5 through 7 provide a more detailed look at the dominant types of real estate partnerships available today, how they work and how they benefit investors.

STEP 4: ESTABLISHING PRIVATE PLACEMENT SUITABILITY

The regulators set an arbitrary standard for "accredited" private placement investors of $200,000 of gross income or a net worth of $1 million. Less wealthy investors can buy in but are limited in number to 35 or fewer in such private placements. However, gross annual income is not nearly as important as other criteria such as discretionary income, predictability of income and type of income. Net worth is an almost meaningless gauge of whether investors are right for partnerships. Discretionary cash flow, liquidity position and personal risk threshold are far more important. The numerical standards may actually be doing investors a disservice.

The investor's personality and attitude toward investing—the "human element"—are important factors in determining "suitability" for private placements. It's critical to determine how the investor feels about such things as illiquid investments, complicated documents and financing arrangements, and the possibility of wrestling with the IRS. Many partnership investments are an act of faith either in the business venture or in the purveyor of the investment.

Furthermore, partnership investment decisions are all too often made one at a time, not with a view toward their overall impact on net worth or the overall composition of the investor's assets. Many professionals feel real estate investing is most productive when executed in the context of total financial and estate planning requirements. Investors and their advisors can only properly judge "suitability" in this perspective.

Matching a real estate partnership's economic benefits with investor needs requires balancing the expected results with those needs. Most partnerships can only maximize one of the available benefits—either cash return, tax shelter or appreciation. Investors and advisors must be realistic regarding the results they expect. Be sure the type of investment selected is designed to accomplish the key objective. And remember, emotional as well as financial "suitability" are a part of fulfilling your expectations.

In hindsight, of course, economically successful investments are suitable for almost anyone. However, assessing economic prospects and risks in partnerships up front can be a tough job, especially for the layman. Risky ventures and extreme leverage are two common causes of economic disaster. Most investors probably should avoid them both. Very few investors understand (much less enjoy) having their investment wiped out, however large the tax benefits they accrue along the way.

Private placements are too often sold like "hot stocks." There's a pressured atmosphere to sign up and pay up. The tax and economic factors are not adequately explained, nor are the ramifications explored. Good private partnerships are hard to find, even though $6 billion worth are sold each year. In this rather large playground, there's a swing with your name on it. Relax. Take the time to study and be conscientious.

Here are seven points for determining true "suitability" for private real estate partnerships (beyond the legal requirements of securities law). Many elements in this checklist are helpful in determining suitability for public real estate offerings as well.

1. **Discretionary Income and Cash Flow**—Most investment-grade partnerships involve cash out-of-pocket. After spending tax dollars, the investor must still lay out cash. So, investors must be willing to draw down personal capital to pay for a partnership, and after-tax income must be greater than personal consumption expenditures. Many relatively high-income executives need tax shelter but don't have the discretionary income to make the investment because "expenses have risen to meet income."

You can borrow in order to buy partnerships. The risk is that the partnership may go astray, and there may be a call for more cash. A strained credit standing may not allow the necessary follow-on investment.

You can cut salary withholding taxes to pay for partnership investments. Partnership losses are a legitimate reason for reducing the amount withheld from paychecks. Investors may file a new W-4 form to reflect the expected reduced tax bill from partnership losses—a good way to help with the cost.

2. **Predictability of Income**—Many real estate partnerships create investment and tax ramifications for many years; some don't. You should match partnerships with individual circumstances. For example, real estate net lease or subsidized housing transactions can generate tax losses for eight or ten years.

Investors with widely fluctuating income are tough candidates for partnership planning (unless, of course, the income fluctuates between "high" and "astronomic"). That's true not just because many partnerships generate losses in later years, but worse, because they may generate large amounts of taxable income in one year. If high personal income and high partnership income years coincide, the combined tax bite can be brutal.

As a general rule, partnership losses should not reduce taxable income below about $60,000 for a joint return ($45,000 single). The reason: Shelter-oriented partnerships are usually priced to produce a reasonable return only if you benefit from tax savings at a high tax rate.

3. **Type Of Income**—For investors seeking to shelter capital gains or make very large charitable contributions, tax losses from partnerships raise a special red flag. Because of the Alternative Minimum Tax created by the Revenue Act of 1978, partnership deductions may only create benefits to the extent of twenty cents on the dollar. This level of benefit can make shelter-oriented partnerships inappropriate and uneconomic.

Too much shelter may also reduce the net tax benefit available. So-called "tax preference items" (such as accelerated depreciation) are subject to the Alternative Minimum Tax.

4. **Liquidity**—Generally accepted wisdom suggests that investors need "adequate" liquid, or marketable, investments before committing funds to partnerships. Certainly, adequate life insurance and medical and disability coverage are priorities. Liquid assets are also necessary to cover contingencies (medical emergencies, a cash cushion for changing jobs, etc.) High write-off partnerships (e.g., real estate net leases and highly leveraged transactions) can build net worth almost entirely with tax savings. So, one could argue there is good sense in pursuing these investments regardless of liquidity.

Older or retired investors must be sure estate tax obligations can be met, and often partnerships should be combined with insurance planning. Sometimes when partnerships pass through estates, appreciation may escape taxes. Real estate partnerships result in a low tax basis for the original purchaser because of depreciation deductions. But, the "stepped-up basis" rules enable the heir to "mark the asset to market value" and establish a new tax basis, effectively eliminating tax on the appreciation.

5. **Risk Threshold**—Private real estate partnerships involve tax, business and timing risks. So, investors shouldn't press too hard to optimize results. Tolerances for loss and uncertainty vary, but one way to reduce risk is to diversify. Buying more

than one kind of partnership and buying partnerships over several years can be very sensible.

If investors are very wealthy and have a large income, they don't need to aggressively seek high financial returns. The combination of risk, leverage and complexity in some private partnerhsips may not be appropriate if the primary interest is preserving capital.

Finally, real estate partnerships can be more risky than you think. Those with the most risk are highly leveraged, single-property transactions where you buy in when the property is under construction or before the property is fully rented.

6. **Human Element**—Partnership investing is different from buying stocks and bonds. Often, investors can't kick and feel what they own, and you certainly can't look up the price in the paper. Partnerships generally distribute lots of reports and financial statements filled with strange words and concepts. Because of accounting practices, these financial statements often don't portray an accurate picture of the economic success or standing of the venture.

Understanding the significance and relevance of complex tax rules adds to the partnership buyer's job and complicates arriving at a "comfort level." Also, factors associated with shelter-oriented partnerships can increase the probability of IRS audit. Some people savour the challenge; some get chills at the thought.

Tax savings from shelter-oriented partnership investments increase disposable income, but these tax savings are hardly ever "saved." With many partnerships, a tag should be placed on those dollars of tax savings identifying their rightful owner— Uncle Sam. Partnership buyers need the discipline to plan for and count on the tax ramifications of partnership ownership in future years—as well as the ability to enjoy the current tax benefits available under our system of taxation.

7. **Planning And Study**—To develop a proper partnership investment strategy, you should analyze personal income, net worth and asset composition on a multi-year basis. The process will focus attention on the ultimate objective of building net

worth, introduce logic (versus emotion) in investment decisions, establish specific objectives, locate capital sources and lead to a plan of action.

Keep the process simple, but look ahead five years. Estimate income, deductions, personal expenditures and any unusual financial requirements, like college tuition. Professional advisors can then plug in the tax and economic consequences of different kinds of real estate partnerships and create an overall investment plan the investor can live with.

Next, concentrate on selecting the kinds and amounts of partnership investments to fit the plan. Implementation is the critical element. "Good" investments will create value. The final step is to select specific partnerships which fit the plan.

The process of planning and study will focus on needs and match them with the benefits real estate partnership investments can reasonably provide. You'll establish realistic goals. Expectations will be geared to likely results. You'll feel a lot more comfortable.

STANGER'S SEVEN-POINT SUITABILITY CHECKLIST FOR PRIVATE REAL ESTATE LIMITED PARTNERSHIPS

1. **DISCRETIONARY INCOME AND CASH FLOW**—Make sure available income is sufficient to fund partnership contributions and an unexpected need for money will not squeeze personal cash.

2. **PREDICTABILITY OF INCOME**—Make sure the partnership's expected tax write-offs and income match personal needs. Widely fluctuating personal income can make multi-year tax write-off partnerships less valuable. Also, watch out for situations where high personal and partnership income may coincide, producing excessive tax liabilities.

3. **TYPE OF INCOME**—Pay attention to Alternative Minimum Tax consequences. Large capital gains generally cannot be sheltered economically.

4. **LIQUIDITY**—Put first things first. In general, liquid assets and adequate insurance are priorities ahead of partnership investments.

5. **RISK THRESHOLD**—Maximizing return with partnerships may not be appropriate for investors who prefer more modest, but certain, returns in their portfolio.

6. **HUMAN ELEMENT**—Make sure complexity, lack of direct control, and increased risk of tax audit are acceptable. Plus, discipline is needed to save tax dollars borrowed "temporarily" from Uncle Sam.

7. **PLANNING AND STUDY**—Develop a strategy for building net worth and consider partnership investments in light of it. Look ahead five years.

CHAPTER 4

DANGERS IN TAX DEALS

There's a tremendous appeal to a real estate transaction in which the annual tax savings are about equal to the annual investment—Uncle Sam pays for the investment. But, as you might suspect, there is no such thing as a "free lunch."

Strictly tax-oriented offerings can be dangerous. Having "no money in the deal" because write-offs are more than twice the cash investment can be a bad deal. Here are some reasons why:

- Residual investment value can be affected by future tax legislation.

- Assets are often overpriced going in.

- High tax brackets may not continue. (An investor may become liable for the Alternative Minimum Tax, a flat tax may be enacted, etc.).

- Financial circumstances may change.

- Accrued tax liability is a real cost.

Investors who can save today (personal spending is less than personal expenses) are much better off with economic real estate transactions. Investors will develop twice the after-tax net worth with economic real estate over the life of the investment compared to strictly tax-oriented real estate.

One investor profile that might benefit from a tax-oriented real estate transaction is a high income, low net worth investor.

Tax-oriented real estate may enable net worth to accumulate largely at Uncle Sam's expense.

BACKGROUND

"Net investment" in a tax-oriented partnership is the amount of money invested in a deal each year less that year's economic benefits—tax credits, tax savings or cash distributions. At any point in time, the amount investors "have in the deal" is cumulative cash investment less cumulative benefits. Typically, capital contributions in privately placed real estate partnerships are staged over three to six years. If cumulative tax losses are two times capital investment during the pay-in period, an investor in the 50% bracket will have "no money in the deal."

In the example below, the first year's benefits are greater than the cash investment, and cash investment and benefits balance out over four years. Investors buy this deal entirely with tax savings. In other words, Uncle Sam pays for the investment.

TAX-ORIENTED PRIVATE PLACEMENT

Year	Investment	Tax Loss	Tax Savings (50% Bracket)	Net Investment (Return)	Cumulative Investment (Return)
1	$ 15,000	$ 42,000	$ 21,000	(6,000)	(6,000)
2	30,000	56,000	28,000	2,000	(4,000)
3	30,000	52,000	26,000	4,000	—
4	25,000	50,000	25,000	—	—
TOTALS	$100,000	$200,000	$100,000	—	—

This way of looking at the cost of the investment only tells part of the story. When you record losses, take tax credits or receive tax-free cash distributions in a partnership investment, you reduce your "tax basis." All such write-downs are recaptured (which means taxed) on sale. When you sell the property, you pay tax on deductions recorded while you owned the property. The amount of the tax you'll owe is a real tax liability. Year by year the amount builds up in most deals. You accumulate a substantial "accrued tax liability."

In the example, if you sold the investment for original cost after four years, you'd have a gain of $200,000. You'd pay $40,000 of tax on the sale, or more, depending on whether the income is capital gain, or fully taxable. With accrued tax liability, investors have to pay Uncle Sam tax to the extent that losses claimed exceed cash investment, even if they lose money on the sale. In the example, you'd owe $20,000 of tax even if your investment were worthless. Here's the way you make the calculation of accrued tax liability:

CALCULATING ACCRUED TAX LIABILITY

Add:	Tax Losses
	Cash Distributions
	Cash Received on Sale
Subtract:	Cash Investment
Result:	Taxable Gain on Sale
Multiply By:	Appropriate Tax Rate

WARNINGS

The major economic benefit in tax-oriented transactions is tax savings in the early years of the investment. Whether the investment makes sense depends, in part, on how tax savings are reinvested (at what rate of return). The higher the rate of return earned on reinvestment, the more a tax-oriented deal benefits the investor. But, for most investors, a lower tax bill from tax savings just increases disposable income. The tax savings are, in fact, never saved and never invested. They are spent.

The total economic benefits during the life of a tax-oriented investment are usually less than $2 per dollar of investment. (Benefits are the cumulative tax savings, cash flow and the residual value of the asset.) Remember, the deal may last for ten to fifteen years. If you were to get back $2 after tax over fifteen years in exchange for a $1 investment now, you would feel cheated. So, obviously net worth is not building up "within" the private placement real estate transaction, but rather "outside" the transaction from reinvestment earnings.

The better answer for many investors may be an "economic" transaction. Here, investors may end up with a value after tax of three to four times original investment in the same ten or fifteen years—twice as much as the tax deal. In effect, the "economic" transaction is a one-decision investment that builds net worth. Here is a comparison of a recent tax-oriented private placement with a typical publicly offered real estate partnership.

COMPARISON OF INVESTMENT RESULTS
IN REAL ESTATE PARTNERSHIPS
(Benefits Per $1 Invested)

	Tax-Oriented Private Placement	Economic Partnership
After-tax Internal Rate of Return	13.8%	13.0%
Economic Benefits	$1.86	$3.20
Residual Value (Cost)	($ .19)	$2.10
Total Economic Benefits Assuming Reinvestment at 8%	$3.20	$3.80

Assuming a 6% increase in rents and expenses, the internal rate of return after tax is about the same for the tax deal and the economic deal. The total economic benefits in the tax deal are $1.86 per dollar of investment versus $3.20 in the economic deal. All the economic benefits come from tax savings in the tax deal versus cash flow and residual value in the economic deal. Two-thirds of the economic benefits are from residual value in the economic deal, whereas taxes due on sale are more than sale proceeds in the tax deal. The economic deal is also better if you assume you reinvest the economic benefits from the transaction at 8% after tax. Adding in reinvestment, the tax deal yields $3.20 per dollar of investment versus $3.80 for the economic deal.

A real estate transaction with high benefits in early years and low benefits over the life of the investment, like a tax deal, can have an internal rate of return equal to or higher than an investment with modest early benefits but significant overall benefits, like the typical economic deal. (For further discussion, See Chapter 20: "Four Ways to Measure Investment Value.")

Which one's best depends on how the investor can reinvest the benefits.

Most investors are probably better off with the economic deal, letting the investment create the value. For one thing, what investors will do with tax savings is not assured. For another, tax deals work only in the highest tax brackets. Remember, financial circumstances change (death, divorce, retirement, etc.). The Alternative Minimum Tax can come into play for many investors—the rate is only 20%. Most "flat tax" proposals call for a top rate of 35% or less. Can you count on a fifteen-year continuation of being in the 50% bracket?

There's a fundamental reason why tax deals are dangerous. Tax-oriented real estate transactions reduce price sensitivity for the sponsor when he's purchasing the property. The higher the price of the asset with increased leverage, the higher the tax deductions. The higher the tax deductions, the more investors are willing to pay. This vicious cycle elevates the price of most tax-oriented real estate private placements beyond reason. We often see transactions where investors have to sell the property for several times the original cost just to break even.

You would think you could always sell the property for at least the original cost to another tax-motivated buyer. This seemingly sensible conclusion may be very far from the truth.When you sell, you'll receive as much as you paid only if the purchaser can benefit from the same tax system from which you benefited. Unfortunately, the 1984 Tax Act changed the rules considerably and reduced tax benefits available for new buyers. Now, the tax deal bought last year is worth less than investors paid for it. Likewise, future legislation may affect the value of current investments.

CHAPTER 5

LEVERAGED REAL ESTATE PARTNERSHIPS

Leveraged real estate should be the cornerstone of a partnership investment portfolio. For one thing, real estate leverage (mortgage debt) is unique because of the amount that can be borrowed and because investors are not personally liable to repay it (the so-called "nonrecourse" feature). Real estate leverage magnifies tax benefits, making leveraged RELPs the only investment allowing a multiple write-off with no personal liability for debt. If all goes well, leverage creates larger investment returns than lack of leverage.

When buying leveraged real estate, the investor's cash investment is a downpayment on income-producing properties. The remainder of the purchase price is borrowed from a lending institution, or in some cases from the seller of the property. The result: Investors have more appreciating assets working per dollar of cash (equity) investment. In real estate private placements, in effect, investors even borrow the equity temporarily because they are often given three to five years to pay in the cash investment. More leverage is available in real estate (most of it at a fixed rate) than for stock margin accounts (at a variable rate). Properties are frequently financed with 75% debt and 25% cash. The maximum which may be borrowed against stocks is generally 50%.

Debt service on real estate leverage usually consists of payments to the lender for interest and principal. Just like the mortgage on a house, over the life of the mortgage the principal payments increase and the interest payments decrease, but the amount of the annual payment is constant. Eventually the mortgage is completely repaid.

The difference between a home mortgage and a mortgage on commercial real estate (office buildings, shopping centers, apartments) is that rental income repays the mortgage on commercial property. Obviously, home mortgage payments require salary or other income.

Since the commercial mortgage is nonrecourse, the lender takes a hard look at the property and calculates the debt coverage ratio (usually around 1.2-to-1). The debt coverage ratio is "net operating income" (rental income less the operating expenses) compared to the annual payment of interest and principal (the mortgage "constant").

So, in real estate whenever investors buy a property with a mortgage, they have, in effect, the lender's view of the value of the property. In most cases, the expected net operating income is sufficiently higher than the mortgage constant for the property to carry itself—i.e., meet all operating expenses and debt payments from the available rental income.

"Equity build-up" can quadruple the investor's money in leveraged real estate with no appreciation in the property. Equity automatically and gradually builds as the mortgage is repaid. For example, suppose you put up $25,000 in cash and buy a $100,000 property with $75,000 of mortgage debt. When the mortgage is fully repaid, your investment will be worth $100,000, or four times the original investment. Debt repayment would take about twenty-five years. But, the expectation of leveraged real estate buyers is to do far better than this.

Relatively modest rates of appreciation produce huge gains in leveraged real estate. Say through good management, good luck or inflation, the property increases in value. At 7% annual appreciation, the $100,000 property grows in value to $200,000 in ten years. By then, the investor has repaid about 15% of the mortgage debt, or approximately $12,000, leaving a debt balance of $63,000. In ten years, your equity is worth $137,000

($200,000 of property value less $63,000 of mortgage balance)—more than five times the original cash investment.

In the U.S. today, the debate isn't over whether there will be inflation or deflation. The argument is over how high inflation will be. Some figure 4% to 6% per annum—others say 7% to 9%. Take your pick, but either guess is well within the range that produces large gains in leveraged real estate for long-term investors.

The nature of leverage and commercial property combine to make long-term holding of real estate the right strategy.Leverage causes initial acquisition expenses to be high in relation to the cash investment. A 6% real estate brokerage (sales) commission on the $100,000 property is $6,000, or 24% of the $25,000 cash down payment. Then, add other closing costs.You can easily see that two or three years of appreciation are necessary to pay for these transaction costs.

Also, in office buildings and shopping centers, tenant leases may run five years or more, although leases probably expire at various times. Management must increase rents for the property to yield more net income, which is the factor that increases property value. With five-year leases, you can only charge more rent every five years. So, you'll have to own the property through several rent turns to increase the value significantly— a long-term proposition.

Holding leveraged real estate long term has proven to be a winning investment strategy.

THE IDEAL TAX SHELTER

The true objective of a tax shelter is to create artificial, not real, losses. If you pay for a tax loss with a cash disbursement, you'd be as well off donating the money to your favorite charity. That's why it makes no sense to describe paying interest or real estate taxes as tax shelters—they are simply deductible business expenses, as are other cash operating expenses of rental property.

But depreciation—that's an entirely different story. You don't pay depreciation in cash although it's an expense for tax purposes. And, if the property holds its value or appreciates, depreciation is a fictional, or artificial, cost.

The concept of depreciation for real property is simple. Eventually, the building will become obsolete, either functionally or economically. Therefore, part of the rental income is a return of capital, or return of your original investment, and should not be taxed when received. The recognition of this concept in the tax code is "depreciation"—Uncle Sam allows you to deduct an amount annually from rental income and keep it tax free to recover your original capital investment. In time, the total of these depreciation deductions will equal the original cost of the building.

With luck, the building will be worth the original cost and maybe more. But, investors take depreciation deductions as though the building is becoming worthless. That's real tax shelter—an artificial loss, one that you don't pay.

Uncle Sam has a way of getting even. When the building is sold, the difference between the "written-down" cost (original cost less cumulative depreciation deductions) and the selling price is taxable gain. Investors still benefit because depreciation deductions save taxes at ordinary tax rates and often the taxable gain is taxed at capital gain rates. Investors benefit further from the time value of money. The depreciation deductions are taken every year investors own the building. The capital gains tax is due only when the building is sold.

Under the tax code, real estate is the only partnership business in which a tax loss can be deductible in excess of cash investment (even if you are not personally liable to repay debt). The limit of loss deductions is your "tax basis" in the property, which begins as your cash investment plus the mortgage debt. Saying the same thing another way, you can depreciate the $100,000 property (assuming all of the property purchase price is attributable to the building) even though you only put up $25,000 of cash.

Here's how investors benefit. With a $25,000 cash downpayment they can either earn $100,000 of rental income entirely tax free (until sale of the property) or, if the property breaks even on a cash basis, they can create $100,000 of "loss" deductions to shelter other income. All the while, the property may be actually appreciating in value. That's leverage and "artificial losses" combined to produce the maximum favorable impact on net worth. Ideal "tax shelter." Ideal investment.

HOW LEVERAGE WORKS

When you borrow money to purchase property, the largest cost component is the mortgage payment. In today's market, you can probably borrow up to 70% of a property's purchase price at a fixed cost. Fixing the cost of the property's largest expense item, interest, results in "financial leverage," which creates an opportunity for big returns.

Suppose you buy $100,000 of property with $30,000 cash down and a 12.3%, 25-year mortgage for $70,000. Here's how things would look during the first five years of operation.

TABLE I
EXAMPLE OF FINANCIAL LEVERAGE

	Year				
	1	2	3	4	5
Rental Income	$14,000	$14,840	$15,730	$16,674	$17,675
Less: Operating Expenses	−4,200	−4,452	−4,719	−5,002	−5,302
Net Operating Income	$ 9,800	$10,388	$11,011	$11,672	$12,373
Less: Debt Service	−9,100	−9,100	−9,100	−9,100	−9,100
Net Cash Flow	$ 700	$ 1,288	$ 1,911	$ 2,572	$ 3,273

NOTE: Assumes rental income and operating expenses increase at an annual rate of 6%; mortgage constant (principal and interest payments) equals 13%.

Financial leverage results in a 47% compound annual increase in net cash flow within five years. That's almost eight times the assumed rate of inflation of 6%! The $700 net cash flow in the first year is about a 2.3% return on the equity downpayment for the property. That's considerably below the $9,800, or 9.8%

return, if the property is bought outright (unleveraged) and no debt payments are required. This is the trade-off inherent in a leveraged investment. You are giving up current return for growth potential. By the fifth year, the financially leveraged investment produces a 10.9% current return on cash investment versus a 12.4% current return on unleveraged ownership. But, your equity in the property has grown from $30,000 to about $56,000, or 87%, in the leveraged deal versus from $100,000 to about $124,000, or 24%, in the unleveraged deal (assuming the property in both cases is worth ten times net operating income). This rapid growth potential makes leveraged real estate the winner for investors seeking capital growth.

At all levels of inflation and property appreciation financial leverage can significantly increase your return. The example below shows the potential effect of leverage on expected after-tax rates of return for a 50% tax bracket investor under six inflation scenarios.

EXAMPLE
AFTER-TAX RATES OF RETURN
LEVERAGED VERSUS UNLEVERAGED REAL ESTATE

	Inflation Scenario					
	0%	2%	4%	6%	8%	10%
Unleveraged	6.5%	7.8%	9.4%	11.1%	12.8%	14.5%
Leveraged	6.9%	10.8%	14.6%	17.9%	21.0%	23.9%

NOTE: Assumptions are the same as those in Table I. Results are at the property level and do not reflect partnership costs and revenue-sharing arrangements.

SOLVING THE CLASSIC INVESTMENT PROBLEM

Leveraged real estate limited partnerships can be the solution to one of the classic investment problems of our time—how to make capital grow faster than inflation. In the last decade, stocks, bonds, Treasury Bills and a variety of other investments have failed this challenge. As we've shown, leveraged RELPs give inflation a four-punch combination knockout:

- Rents and operating profits tend to increase with inflation.

Income-producing property values are a multiple of operating profits, so inflation translates into capital appreciation.

- "Leveraging" a real estate investment with mortgage borrowing magnifies potential return. Real after-tax rates of return from leveraged RELPs can be about twice the rate of inflation.
- Leverage provides better tax benefits.
- At either low or high inflation rates, leveraged income-producing properties can provide superior returns compared with other investments.

A typical pro forma financial projection of a leveraged public RELP is shown on the next page.

ILLUSTRATION: THE ANSWER FOR TUITION TRAUMA

Here's an example of how periodic investment in leveraged public RELPs can build a substantial nest egg for future college tuition bills.

Room, board and tuition costs for U.S. colleges average more than $10,000 per year in a private school. At an inflation rate of 7% per annum, ten years from now the cost will be nearly $20,000 per year, or $80,000 to pay for a four-year college degree. What's worse, parents have to come up with the cash after taxes.

By investing $5,000 a year for ten years in the typical real estate limited partnership (and reinvesting the cash flow and tax savings during the period), an investor can create a stream of after-tax cash distributions totaling $245,000 (assuming 7% annual inflation) from the tenth through the twentieth year. Approximately $25,000 per annum after tax should be enough for several college educations, even at tomorrow's inflated costs.

The higher inflation pushes tuition expenses, the larger the cash distributions from the real estate investment should grow.

TABLE II
LEVERAGED REAL ESTATE PARTNERSHIP MODEL—RETURN PER $10,000 INVESTED

	Operating Phase									
	Year									
	1	2	3	4	5	6	7	8	9	10
Property Rental Income	$3,401	$3,639	$3,894	$4,167	$4,458	$4,771	$5,105	$5,462	$5,844	$6,253
Less Operating Expense	−1,259	−1,347	−1,441	−1,542	−1,650	−1,765	−1,889	−2,021	−2,162	−2,314
Net Operating Income	2,142	2,292	2,453	2,625	2,808	3,006	3,216	3,441	3,682	3,939
Less: Debt Service	−1,602	−1,602	−1,602	−1,602	−1,602	−1,602	−1,602	−1,602	−1,602	−1,602
Cash to Partnership	540	690	851	1,023	1,206	1,404	1,614	1,839	2,080	2,337
Less Partnership Expenses	− 200	− 214	− 229	− 245	− 262	− 280	− 300	− 321	− 343	− 368
Distributable Cash	340	476	622	778	944	1,124	1,314	1,518	1,736	1,969
Less: GP Fees	− 13	− 18	− 23	− 29	− 80	− 159	− 99	− 114	− 130	− 148
Pretax Return to Limited Partners	$ 327	$ 458	$ 599	$ 749	$ 864	$ 965	$1,215	$1,404	$1,606	$1,821
Current Pretax Yield	3.3%	4.6%	6.0%	7.5%	8.6%	9.7%	12.2%	14.0%	16.1%	18.2%
Tax Savings (Cost)	$ 460	$ 460	$ 381	$ 307	$ 227	$ (55)	$(148)	$(247)	$(353)	$(467)
Total After-Tax Benefits to LP Per $10,000	$ 787	$ 918	$ 980	$1,056	$1,091	$ 910	$1,067	$1,157	$1,253	$1,354
Current After-Tax Yield	7.9%	9.2%	9.8%	10.6%	10.9%	9.1%	10.7%	11.6%	12.5%	13.5%

Liquidation Phase (000's)

Gross Sale Proceeds	$42,153
Less: Mortgage Balance Due	− 12,758
Less: Disposition Fee	− 1,265
Less: GP Participation	− 2,720
LP Sale Proceeds	$25,410
Plus: Return of Reserves	1,298
LP Liquidation Proceeds	$26,708
Less: Taxes Due on Sale	− 4,929
LP After-Tax Proceeds	$21,779

Total Return

	Pretax	After-Tax
Original Investment	$10,000	$10,000
Cash Flow During Operating Phase	10,009	10,009
Cash Flow at Liquidation	26,708	21,779
Total Return	$36,717	$32,353
Total Return/Investment Ratio	3.7/1	3.2/1
Internal Rate of Return	16%	15.6%

NOTES: Table based on a $10 million partnership purchasing $21.4 million of existing, income-producing properties with $7.5 million cash down payment and an 11%, 30-year mortgage from the seller (65% leverage). Property depreciated using straight-line method. 80% of purchase price is allocated to building, 10% to personal property and 10% to land. Property purchased and sold at a 10% capitalization rate. Partnership offering terms are rated AA (see Chapter 13). After-tax returns are for a 44% tax bracket investor assuming 7% annual appreciation.

That's the interesting thing about selecting a leveraged real estate investment program to meet this particular financial obligation. For instance, at a 10% inflation rate, after-tax cash distributions would grow to more than $400,000, or an average of $40,000 annually.

Selecting "leveraged" real estate as the investment vehicle increases the spread between after-tax cash distributions and tuition payments. For instance, a 10% inflation rate will increase annual tuition costs in the tenth year from $20,000 to $26,000, an increase of 30%. But, this higher inflation rate for real estate will increase cash distributions in the tenth year from $18,000 to $30,000, an increase of over 60%.

Real estate limited partnerships have a significant edge over zero coupon bonds ("zeros"), a popular investment suggested by financial advisors to fund future tuition expenses. (Zero coupon bonds are issued at a substantial discount from par value or redemption price. The bonds pay no current interest in cash. A part of the discount from redemption value is taxed to the holder annually as accrued interest.) In many cases, parents purchase zeros in a child's name to avoid the tax liability on the interest accrual. Or, alternatively, they buy tax-free zeros.

A 10% tax-free zero purchased for $5,000 will be redeemed at about $13,000 in ten years. A ten-year purchase program in municipal zeros costing $50,000 will generate $127,000 in future value after tax, about one-half the value of a similar real estate investment program.

The advantage of real estate over taxable zeros can be even greater. There's an additional advantage in real estate. Due to the combination of tax loss deductions (tax savings) and tax sheltered cash flow, the parents can keep the real estate investment in their name and not seriously reduce the family's net financial return after tax. On the other hand, parents must gift the zeros to children irrevocably to keep from being eaten alive with taxes on accrued interest.

Giving away the zeros has another disadvantage beside loss of control of the funds. The child may be ineligible for certain types of scholarships. Generally, the student must utilize his own net worth (which would include the value of the zeros) to pay school bills before he is eligible for many types of financial aid.

Table III on the next page summarizes results of investing $5,000 each year in real estate limited partnerships for ten years assuming different levels of appreciation (inflation) compared to a $5,000 annual investment in 10% municipal zeros or 14% taxable zeros.

As you can see from the comparisons, the ratio of return to investment is at least twice as high for the leveraged real estate investments as for either zero coupon bond. Over ten years, real estate partnerships can return five to eight times the amount invested, depending on the inflation rate. The maximum return from the zeros is about two-and-a-half times investment. The internal rate of return after tax is at least 60% greater for real estate. Assuming a 10% inflation rate, the after-tax internal rate of return in real estate is more than 21% per annum, almost twice the after-tax internal rate of return on the zeros. The net after-tax investment in the real estate is always less.

If parents start this investment plan when their oldest child is five, they have an added bonus—they can get back the original principal and still afford tuition. For example, at 7% inflation the tax savings and cash distributions from the tenth through the twelfth years of the plan (when the child is 15 through 17 years old) will equal $61,997—more than the original investment. What's more, $183,145 will still be available for tuition.

TABLE III
INVESTMENT COMPARISON
Invest $5,000 Each Year For Ten Years

	Real Estate Partnerships				Zero Coupon Bonds	
	With Cash Flow Reinvested		With Cash Flow And Tax Savings Reinvested			
	7% Appreciation	10% Appreciation	7% Appreciation	10% Appreciation	10% Municipal	14% Taxable
Original Investment	$ 50,000	$ 50,000	$ 50,000	$ 50,000	$ 50,000	$ 50,000
Tax (Savings) Cost Not Reinvested	(5,905)	(5,924)	0	0	0	19,250
Out-of-Pocket Cash Investment	$ 44,095 (1)	$ 44,076 (1)	$ 50,000 (1)	$ 50,000 (1)	$ 50,000	$ 69,250
Total After-Tax Benefits (10th through 20th year) (2)	$218,461	$357,010	$245,142	$401,328	$126,960	$177,730 (3)
Ratio of Return to Investment (after-tax)	5.0:1	8.1:1	4.9:1	8.0:1	2.5:1	2.6:1
Internal Rate of Return	16.8%	21.6%	16.8%	22.1%	10.0%	10.7%

(1) In addition, cash reinvested after tax from cash flow during the first ten years is $33,425 in the 7% appreciation case and $44,643 in the 10% appreciation case. Reinvested tax savings total $7,575 and $6,357 respectively in the 7% and 10% appreciation cases.

(2) Assumes partnerships are liquidated ratably from seventh through eleventh years after partnership formation.

(3) Redemption value less tax on interest accruing after year ten.

NOTES: Assumes "standard" costs of partnerships for front-end fees (20%), operational phase fees (5% of distributable cash) and liquidation phase fees (3% commission on sale price plus 10% of gain over original cost). Assumes tax savings (or cost) in the 50% bracket and capital gains taxes at 20%.

CHAPTER 6

UNLEVERAGED REAL ESTATE PARTNERSHIPS

To keep borrowing costs down, you can pay all cash to buy properties. This technique results in an "unleveraged" real estate limited partnership. Unleveraged partnerships borrow no money, pay no debt service and offer competitive current yield and growth potential in both income and capital. So, they are a hot item on Wall Street for both Individual Retirement Accounts (IRAs) and taxable investors.

Unleveraged real estate partnerships are good investments for investors seeking both income growth and capital growth virtually risk free. Debt-free real estate produces a healthy income stream (65% operating profit margins or better) which is partially sheltered from taxes by property depreciation. As rental income rises, property value also rises, resulting in a capital gain when the property is sold.

A $10,000 investment in a typical unleveraged limited partnership can return original investment plus $15,000 before taxes over the life of the investment if rents appreciate 7% each year. First-year pretax cash return can be around 8% (two-thirds sheltered by property depreciation). Unleveraged partnerships can generate pretax internal rates of return in the 12%-15% range, and after-tax rates of return of 10% to 12%.

The table on the next page shows the projected returns for an actual unleveraged partnership offering. For each $10,000 invested, $8,250 is left to buy property after front-end fees. An additional $200 is set aside as a partnership cash reserve. The

UNLEVERAGED REAL ESTATE PARTNERSHIP MODEL
RETURN PER $10,000 INVESTED

Operating Phase

						Year				
	1	2	3	4	5	6	7	8	9	10
Pretax Return to LP	$ 757	$ 810	$ 867	$ 928	$ 992	$1,062	$1,136	$1,216	$1,253*	$1,317*
Current Pretax Yield	7.6%	8.1%	8.7%	9.3%	9.9%	10.6%	11.4%	12.2%	12.5%	13.2%*
Tax Cost (Savings)	$ 75	$ 75	$ 101	$ 126	$ 152	$ 244	$ 274	$ 307	$ 342	$ 379
After-tax Return to LP	$ 682	$ 735	$ 766	$ 802	$ 840	$ 818	$ 862	$ 909	$ 911*	$ 938*
Current After-tax Yield	6.8%	7.4%	7.7%	8.0%	8.4%	8.2%	8.6%	9.1%	9.1%*	9.4%*

Liquidation Phase

Pretax Sale Proceeds to LP	$14,451
Less: Taxes Due On Sale	−1,418
After-tax Sale Proceeds to LP	$13,033

Total Return

	Pretax	After-tax
Original Investment	$10,000	$10,000
Cash Flow During Operating Phase	10,338	8,263
Cash Flow at Liquidation	14,451	13,033
Total Return	$24,789	$21,296
Total Return/Investment Ratio	2.5/1	2.1/1
Internal Rate of Return	12.3%	10.0%

NOTES: Table assumes rental income and expenses increase 7% per annum. Tax consequences assume 38% tax bracket. 80% of purchase price allocated to building, 10% to personal property and 10% to land. Building depreciated using straight-line method. Partnership offering terms are rated AA (see Chapter 13).

* Deferred GP Operating phase fees are taken in years nine and ten.

portfolio generates $805 in cash flow to the partnership in the first year. Partnership expenses reduce distributable cash to $757, or 7.6% of original investment. In some deals, the general partner agrees to defer payment of his share of distributable cash until limited partners receive a stated yield. In our example, the general partner defers his operating phase fee until investors receive a 10% yield. Yearly income will grow as rents increase. Each year a 5% to 6% return is sheltered by property depreciation, the rest is taxable.

In year ten, property appreciation results in pretax sale proceeds to the limited partners of $14,451 per $10,000 investment. Overall, the pretax return from operations and sale proceeds equals almost $25,000 on a $10,000 investment, and the pretax internal rate of return is over 12%.

For a taxable investor in the 38% bracket, first-year return after tax is 6.8%, growing to 9.4% in the tenth year. After-tax sale proceeds are over $13,000 per $10,000 invested. Overall, the after-tax return from operations and sale proceeds exceeds $21,000 on a $10,000 investment, and the after-tax internal rate of return is 10%.

CHAPTER 7

PARTICIPATING MORTGAGE PARTNERSHIPS

Participating mortgage real estate partnerships can provide competitive current cash yields, the opportunity for principal appreciation and relatively low risk. These partnerships provide mortgage financing to existing and developing real estate projects in excess of the amount available from conventional lending sources. In exchange, the partnership receives and passes through the current income from interest payments and additional interest (the "participation") from a percentage of increased cash flow of the property and/or a portion of the appreciation. These investments make sense for investors who want current income. Since they are relatively safe and offer rates competitive with or higher than bank CD rates, they also are attractive investments for IRAs, Keogh plans, or other tax-exempt accounts.

At today's mortgage loan rates, investors can probably obtain a current annual cash return initially of about 8% to 9% net of partnership costs and fees. This annual cash flow can grow to over 14% in ten years. Upon sale or refinancing of the property, the repayment of the mortgage plus the participation in the appreciation can amount to over 150% of initial investment. At 7% appreciation per annum, total dollar returns over the ten-year life of the partnership can exceed $2.50 (annual interest plus additional interest) for each dollar invested. Of course, the actual result depends in part upon the rate of appreciation for the property financed and the partnership's share of the growth in property value.

The downside? As a mortgage lender, the investor's minimum return should be the repayment of principal plus interest at the stated rate. The investment is secured by a property with probably 15% to 25% more value than the amount of the loan.

BACKGROUND

There are two primary methods of investing in income-producing real estate—equity investment and mortgage lending. An equity investor buys the property (perhaps with the aid of mortgage financing) and receives any income remaining after the payment of operating expenses and mortgage payments. Depreciation deductions will shelter the cash return to a certain extent. The equity investor assumes all the operating risks but receives all the financial rewards as well. If operating cash flow enjoys healthy growth, the equity investor will obtain high annual cash returns and will also benefit fully from the appreciation of the property's value when it is sold.

Mortgage lenders, on the other hand, typically seek a fixed annual return. Conventional mortgage lenders do not receive any of the tax benefits from ownership or any of the increase in cash flow or appreciation. Mortgage loan rates typically exceed current cash returns equity owners will accept. Usually the principal amount of the mortgage loan does not exceed 75% of the value of the property.

Participating mortgage loans earn a fixed rate of interest and an "equity kicker"—a share of any future increase in cash flow and/or participation in the value of the property when it is sold or refinanced. In exchange for this equity participation, the mortgage partnership lends at a base rate of interest which is slightly below the prevailing market rate and generally lends a higher percentage of property value than is available with a conventional fixed-rate mortgage.

One gauge of the relative safety of mortgage loans is the "loan-to-value ratio," the percentage of a property's value which is accounted for by the mortgage indebtedness. The lower the loan-to-value ratio, the higher the property value in relation to the mortgage amount and the greater the safety for mortgage lenders. Today, the typical loan-to-value ratio for participating mortgage loans is 75% to 85%—the partnership would be willing to make a mortgage loan for $750,000 to $850,000 for a property valued at $1 million. This percentage is greater than the major institutions lend (such as insurance companies and pension funds) for fixed rate mortgages.

Today's participating mortgages start with a base interest rate about 1% to 2% below conventional mortgages. In some, rates are lower in the early years, and then, as property economics improve, the base rate increases gradually. Payments on participating mortgages are generally for interest only, with the original principal amount due in ten years.

Of course, the base interest rate depends on the size of the equity kicker. The larger the kicker, the lower the rate. For example, a typical formula might call for 25% participation in all rental income increases over scheduled base amounts plus 40% of sale or refinancing proceeds (or increases in the appraised value of the property) after repayment of the underlying mortgage. A participating mortgage can earn as much as 20% to 50% of the increase in cash flow and up to 50% of the appreciation.

PARTICIPATING "FIRSTS" VERSUS "SECONDS"

Investors can choose between participating "first" or "second" mortgage loan funds, depending on their willingness to assume extra risk for greater capital growth potential. Participating first mortgage loan funds lend money to developers and buyers of existing property and receive a fixed rate of interest plus a "participation" in cash flow and property appreciation. In today's market, participating first mortgage funds typically lend 75% of a property's value and receive about 11% annual interest plus almost 40% of net operating income increases. When the property is sold, the fund typically receives 40% of any equity gain, all of which is considered ordinary interest, taxable at ordinary rates.

Participating second mortgage funds lend money on a property already subject to first mortgage debt—usually older buildings with favorable (low-rate) first mortgages. The favorable rate on the first mortgage blends with the higher rate on the second mortgage to give the borrower a reasonable combined debt service cost.

The participating "second" is riskier than a participating "first" because the second mortgage lender's claim on the property's net operating income and the underlying collateral is subordinated to the interest of the first mortgage holder. Sometimes, the second mortgage lender will defer a portion of the interest payments until the property generates sufficent cash to pay the additional debt service on the second mortgage. Participating second mortgage loan funds typically lend between 20% and 50% of property value. The combined financing provided by participating first and second mortgage loans can total up to 85% of property value. In exchange for these risks, participating second mortgage lenders receive a higher fixed rate of interest and a higher dollar-for-dollar participation in rent and property appreciation than the participating first mortgage lender.

To take a participating second mortgage, the borrower must benefit compared to taking a loan from a nonparticipating lender. The benefit could be a larger loan amount (a higher loan-to-value ratio). Other benefits could be a longer time until the loan is due (maturity), or a lower interest rate in the early years. On the other hand, the lender hopes the participation in rent increases and property appreciation will push his overall rate of return higher.

ECONOMIC BENEFITS

Three factors influence return from participating mortgage partnerships: (1) the terms of the mortgage loans; (2) the economic performance of the property; and (3) the cost and revenue sharing arrangements between limited and general partners.

The tables on the following pages show hypothetical results of "first" and "second" mortgage loan partnership investments over ten years. The results are based on property acquisition projections and deal structures for two participating mortgage loan partnerships.

During the operating phase, cash flow comes from fixed interest payments plus participations in increases in rental income over a base amount. When the borrower repays the loan, the partnership receives the principal amount of the loan and a share of the excess sale or refinancing proceeds above the loan amount. At the partnership level, upon repayment of the mortgage, funds are paid out as follows: (1) to the limited partners up to the amount of original investment; (2) to the limited partners until they achieve a "preferential" return (i.e., a noncompounded cumulative annual return on their adjusted capital accounts); (3) to the general partners as real estate commissions; (4) to the limited partners and the general partners, often on an 85%/15% formula, until all the remaining proceeds are distributed.

A $10,000 investment in the typical participating first mortgage partnership will return almost $24,000 over 10 years assuming annual appreciation of 7%. (See Table I on page 61.) That's a 12% pretax internal rate of return. What's more, the current yield is a healthy 9% in the first year increasing to about 13% over the life of the investment. Over the first seven years, returns average slightly below 10%. If the property appreciates, investors lock in a very competitive rate of return. And, even if the property fails to appreciate, the pretax internal rate of return on the investment exceeds 10%.

Sure, it may be less than a bond. But look again. At the end of ten years you can get back around 130% of your original investment. That's appreciation and the equity kicker at work. All you get back with a bond is the return of your principal.

Table II on page 62 shows hypothetical results for a partnership holding participating second mortgages. At the time the property is refinanced, investors receive almost $15,000 per $10,000 invested. Investors receive a total of nearly $26,000 over the term of the loan per $10,000 of investment, a 13.0% pretax internal rate of return.

Participating mortgage loan partnerships probably aren't the best bet for taxable investors. Income is not sheltered as with other types of real estate investments and the kicker appreciation amount is considered "additional interest" taxable as ordinary income rather than as capital gain. The next chapter examines investment return based on tax bracket and helps you determine which type of "income-oriented" partnership will maximize investment return.

TABLE I
PARTICIPATING FIRST MORTGAGE LOAN PARTNERSHIP MODEL
RETURN PER $10,000 INVESTED

	Operating Phase					Year				
	1	2	3	4	5	6	7	8	9	10
Net Return to LP	$ 906	$ 950	$ 964	$ 969	$ 988	$1,051	$1,103	$1,152	$1,204	$1,259
Current Yield	9.1%	9.5%	9.6%	9.7%	9.9%	10.5%	11.0%	11.5%	12.0%	12.6%

Repayment Phase

(1) Property Selling Price (or Appraised Value)	$23,344
(2) Less: Loan Repayment	8,900
(3) Return of Equity Owner's Capital	2,967
	$11,477
	x .4
(4) Partnership Participation (40%)	$ 4,591
(5) Total to Mortgage Partnership (2+4)	$13,491
(6) Less: GP Incentive Fee	524
(7) Total Sale Proceeds to LP	$12,967

Total Return

Original Investment	$10,000
Cash Flow During Operating Phase	10,546
Cash Flow at Repayment	12,967
Total Return	$23,513
Total Return/Investment Ratio	2.4/1
Pretax Internal Rate of Return	11.9%

NOTES: Table assumes a $10 million partnership makes an $8.9 million participating first mortgage loan on an $11.9 million residential property (loan-to-value ratio equals 75%). Annual mortgage payments are interest only with principal due in ten years. The base interest rate begins at 11%, escalating to 13% in the sixth year. Equity participation during the operating phase is 25% of all gross rental income over a scheduled base amount. Participation upon property sale or refinancing equals 40% of excess proceeds over the loan amount plus the equity owner's original capital. Property rents and expenses increase 7% per annum. Partnership offering terms are rated AA (see Chapter 13). Results shown are for a tax-exempt investor (e.g., IRA or Keogh plan).

TABLE II
PARTICIPATING SECOND MORTGAGE LOAN PARTNERSHIP MODEL
RETURN PER $10,000 INVESTED

| | Operating Phase Returns | | | | | | | | | |
| | | | | | Year | | | | | |
	1	2	3	4	5	6	7	8	9	10
Net Return to LP	$824	$856	$889	$1,032	$1,071	$1,112	$1,156	$1,310	$1,361	$1,414
Current Yield	8.2%	8.6%	8.9%	10.3%	10.7%	11.1%	11.6%	13.1%	13.6%	14.1%

Repayment Phase

Total Sale Proceeds to Partnership	$15,933
Less: GP Return of Capital And Commissions	– 518
GP Incentive Fee	– 593
Total Sale Proceeds to LP	$14,822

Total Return

Original Investment	$10,000
Cash Flow During Operating Phase	11,025
Cash Flow at Repayment	14,822
Total Return	$25,847
Total Return/Investment Ratio	2.6/1
Pretax Internal Rate of Return	13.0%

NOTES: Table assumes a $10 million partnership makes an $8.9 million participating second mortgage loan on an $18.7 million property subject to an $8 million first mortgage balance with a 10.1% debt service constant. Participation during the operating phase equals 15% of gross rents over a scheduled base amount. Participation upon property sale or refinancing equals ten times the maximum annual participation in gross rents. Property rents and expenses increase 7% per annum. Partnership offering terms are rated AA (see Chapter 13). Results shown are for a tax-exempt investor (e.g., IRA or Keogh plan).

CHAPTER 8

CHOOSING THE RIGHT TYPE OF INCOME-ORIENTED REAL ESTATE PARTNERSHIP

Income-oriented real estate partnerships (unleveraged equity and mortgage loan funds) have emerged as the overwhelming choice of today's partnership investors. By stressing current income with capital growth potential, these partnerships are especially attractive for the rapidly growing IRA market as well as for taxable investors. Total investment in income-oriented RELPs exploded from $800 million in 1982 to $4.6 billion in 1985. Almost 70 cents of every dollar invested in publicly registered RELPs now goes to income-oriented partnerships, double the rate in 1982.

The type of income-oriented real estate partnership that is right for an investor depends on his tax bracket and inflation expectation. Tax-exempt investors probably maximize return by investing in participating second (or wraparound) mortgage loan funds. Typical participating "seconds" (or wraps) generally provide higher rates of return than participating first mortgage loan funds and unleveraged equity funds.

For taxable investors, unleveraged equity funds are the best bet. At 10% annual inflation or higher, unleveraged equity is also the best bet for tax-exempt investors.

If you are concerned about inflation, all three types of income-oriented real estate investments provide a "real" (inflation-adjusted) return to tax-exempt investors even at high rates of inflation. That's proof of real estate's fundamental investment merit in all economic conditions, and that's why real estate should be a part of every pension or retirement portfolio.

To see how projected returns compare under a variety of economic scenarios, three partnerships were reviewed—unleveraged equity, participating first mortgage loan and participating second mortgage loan. All three programs received identical Stanger Offering Terms Ratings (see Chapter 13) signifying that the share of return net to the limited partner in each is comparable.

Of course, the actual investment result from a real estate limited partnership depends on the income-producing potential of the underlying property and the expertise of the general partner. An unleveraged equity fund investor benefits directly from the general partner's ability to acquire quality properties at the best price, manage them efficiently, and sell them at the right time. A participating mortgage investor benefits from interest payments and "participation" in increases in property income and value. Here, the investor relies on the general partner to finance properties with high income potential and negotiate the highest percentage participation and loan interest rate. Sponsors with superior selection and negotiation skills can put more money into investors' pockets. So, the investment result from alternative income-oriented investments depends in part on the sponsor you select. (Section IV explains how to evaluate the sponsor organization.)

RESULTS FOR TAX-EXEMPT INVESTORS

Tax-exempt investors can expect the highest returns from participating second (or wraparound) mortgage loan funds when annual inflation is less than 10%. Internal rates of return average 11.1% for the unleveraged equity fund, 11.2% for the participating first mortgage fund, and 12.3% for the participating second mortgage loan fund when annual inflation ranges between 1% and 10%. (See Table I.) At rates of inflation below 6%, both "first" and second" mortgage loan investments produce tax-exempt returns superior to the unleveraged equity fund.

TABLE I
COMPARISON OF INTERNAL RATES OF RETURN
TO TAX-EXEMPT INVESTORS

Annual Inflation	Unleveraged Equity Fund	Participating 1st Mortgage Loan Fund	Participating 2nd Mortgage Loan Fund
1%	7.6%	9.1%	10.2%
2%	8.5%	9.5%	10.6%
3%	9.2%	9.9%	11.0%
4%	9.8%	10.4%	11.5%
5%	10.6%	10.8%	11.9%
6%	11.4%	11.4%	12.4%
7%	12.3%	11.9%	13.0%
8%	13.1%	12.5%	13.5%
9%	13.9%	13.0%	14.1%
10%	**14.8%**	13.6%	14.7%
Averages	11.1%	11.2%	12.3%
Ranges	7.6%–14.8%	9.1%–13.6%	10.2%–14.7%

NOTES: Table assumes property appreciation equals the inflation rate. Results based on projections and actual deal terms of three publicly registered limited partnerships. Offering terms are all rated "AA" signifying that the limited partner's share of net return is comparable for each partnership (see Chapter 13).

At high rates of inflation, the unleveraged equity fund typically produces the best return in an IRA or Keogh account. With annual inflation of 10%, the internal rate of return from the unleveraged equity fund is 14.8% versus 13.6% for the participating "first" and 14.7% for the participating "second." At higher rates of inflation, the advantage of the unleveraged equity fund increases.

Even if inflation reaches 10% annually, all three investments produce positive "real" (inflation-adjusted) rates of return of about 4% or more. And, they continue to provide "real" rates of return at 16% annual inflation. That's effective inflation protection for retirement portfolios.

For investors seeking maximum safety, the participating first mortgage loan program is probably most appropriate. Even in a deflationary economy in which property income declines, limited partners receive an internal rate of return of about 9% from the participating "first"—about one-and-a-half times what a typical unleveraged equity fund pays. Participating "seconds" also protect investors from adverse swings in property values and income. But, to the extent that loan-to-value ratios are increased with second mortgage financing, declining property income may result in insufficient funds to pay the interest (and accruals) due on the second mortgage. In exchange for the safety of the preferred position of a "first" lender, investors receive a rate of return about 1% lower in a participating "first" mortgage loan fund than in a participating "second" regardless of tax bracket or the rate of inflation.

RESULTS FOR TAXABLE INVESTORS

For investors in the 38% tax bracket or more, expected return is highest in the unleveraged equity fund. Internal rates of return average 9.0% for the unleveraged equity fund, 7.2% for the participating first mortgage fund, and 8.3% for the participating second mortgage fund when annual inflation ranges from 1% to 10%. The unleveraged equity fund outperforms both types of mortgage loan funds under all inflation scenarios above 2%. When adjusted for inflation, returns from the unleveraged equity fund remain the highest. (See Table II below.)

TABLE II
COMPARISON OF AFTER-TAX INTERNAL RATES OF RETURN TO INVESTOR IN 38% TAX BRACKET

Annual Inflation	Unleveraged Equity Fund	Participating 1st Mortgage Loan Fund	Participating 2nd Mortgage Loan Fund
1%	6.0%	5.5%	**6.6%**
2%	6.8%	5.9%	**6.9%**
3%	**7.4%**	6.2%	7.3%
4%	**7.9%**	6.5%	7.6%
5%	**8.5%**	6.9%	8.0%
6%	**9.2%**	7.3%	8.4%
7%	**10.0%**	7.7%	8.9%
8%	**10.7%**	8.1%	9.3%
9%	**11.5%**	8.6%	9.8%
10%	**12.2%**	9.0%	10.3%
Averages	9.0%	7.2%	8.3%
Ranges	6.0%–12.2%	5.5%–9.0%	6.6%–10.3%

NOTE: Assumptions same as in Table I.

Only the unleveraged equity fund gives the high tax bracket investor positive real return at high inflation levels. The inflation-adjusted return from the participating first mortgage loan fund becomes negative when annual inflation exceeds 8%. With the participating second mortgage loan fund, inflation wins when it hits 11%. But, investors get a real economic gain with the unleveraged equity fund investment in all inflation scenarios.

CHAPTER 9

"FREITs": AN ALTERNATIVE TO LIMITED PARTNERSHIPS

Finite-life (self-liquidating) real estate investment trusts ("FREITs") are an appealing alternative as a vehicle for real estate investing. FREITs have most of the benefits of limited partnerships. Both investment vehicles:

- pool investor funds to purchase or finance a diversified portfolio of income-producing properties;
- pay out cash flow and cash distributions directly;
- preserve the investor's limited liability;
- are not subject to tax; and
- eventually sell the properties and distribute the cash.

FREITs have several advantages over limited partnerships. First, they solve one of the most common objections to limited partnership investments—lack of liquidity. If you have to sell a limited partnership investment, finding a buyer can be difficult. And, the price you negotiate may be significantly discounted from the value of the partnership's underlying assets.

Shares in a FREIT are traded in secondary markets. So, you have a choice—use the liquidity of a secondary market or wait to receive the full value of the investment when the portfolio of properties is sold and the cash is distributed. FREITs also provide greater control over the sponsor, and you are given an appraised value of the investment—not true in typical limited partnerships.

Investors seeking tax shelter should stick with partnerships. While the cash flow from FREITs is partially tax sheltered by depreciation, investors cannot use FREIT losses to offset other income. FREITs are particularly well suited for tax-exempt investors—from big institutional pension funds to "little guy" participants in IRAs and Keogh Plans. FREITs provide current cash flow as the primary benefit. But, unlike bonds, the income stream can grow, and the principal value of the investment can increase. In addition, FREITs allow pension plans to seek more aggressive growth through the use of leverage without incurring "unrelated business taxable income."

ADVANTAGES OVER LIMITED PARTNERSHIPS

FREITs provide many of the benefits of limited partnerships: diversified portfolios, access to investment grade properties for small investors, real estate management expertise, limited liability, avoidance of the double taxation inherent in investments in real estate corporations, and combinations of current cash flow and appreciation potential. But, there are important differences. (See Table I on the next page.)

The greatest advantage FREITs offer over limited partnerships is liquidity. Organized secondary trading markets do not exist for limited partnership interests. You'll have to find your own buyer. (Usually, the general partner or brokerage house can refer you to potential buyers.) Unfortunately, the price you negotiate can be considerably below the fair market value of the partnership unit. In contrast, FREIT "shares of beneficial interest" are traded in secondary markets—on the New York Stock Exchange, American Stock Exchange or in the Over-the-Counter market.

Investors can tell how their investment is doing more easily with a FREIT than with a typical limited partnership. That's because FREIT trustees are required to have independent property appraisals annually. Limited partnerships are only required to do so to qualify under ERISA for pension fund and other tax-deferred retirement plan investors.

TABLE I
COMPARISON OF FREITs WITH LIMITED PARTNERSHIPS

	Finite-Life REIT	Limited Partnership
Limited Liability for Investor	Yes	Yes
Diversified Portfolio of Investment-Grade Properties	Yes	Yes
Professional Management	Yes	Yes
Equity and/or Mortgage Investments	Yes	Yes
Single Level of Taxation	Yes	Yes
Liquidity	Yes	No
Minimum Investment Amount	As Low As $18	Generally $2,000
Ability to Leverage Without Incurring UBTI for Tax-Exempt Accounts	Yes	No
Provides Tax Shelter Via Pass-through of Losses	No	Yes
Investor Control Over Sponsor	Investors Re-elect Trustees and Retain Advisors Annually	Removal of GP Difficult
Required Annual Appraisals	Yes	Only When ERISA Qualified

Investors have greater control over management in a FREIT than in a limited partnership. FREIT trustees are elected by shareholders annually, and advisors (generally, the sponsor organization) are retained subject to annual review. In a partnership, removal of the general partner can be difficult.

FREITs also provide greater portfolio flexibility. Minimum investment amounts are quite small, and investors can easily increase or reduce their holdings through the secondary market.

Finally, pension funds and tax-exempt investors can pursue appreciation more aggressively through FREITs than limited partnerships. The reason: A special IRS ruling exempts REIT distributions earned via leveraged holdings from taxation as "unrelated business taxable income" ("UBTI"). In contrast, leveraged limited partnerships may create UBTI which is taxable even to pension funds. (UBTI above $1,000 is subject to tax.)

REITs

REITs were created by Congress in 1960 to give the small investor an opportunity to share in the ownership of investment-grade properties or in the profits of mortgage lending. (FREITs are a variety of REITs and are taxed and regulated identically.) Congress exempted REITs from corporate taxation if the trusts: (1) maintain at least 75% of assets in some combination of real estate equity, mortgages secured by real property, and cash or government securities; (2) derive at least 75% of gross income from real estate operations; (3) distribute at least 95% of annual net income to shareholders; (4) refrain from quick asset turnover; (5) have at least 100 shareholders, with holdings spread widely enough to restrict insider domination; and (6) retain independent professional experts and trustees for stipulated fiduciary and managerial functions.

If REITs meet these requirements income is not taxed to the REIT but is taxed only once, when investors receive it—the same as partnerships. Unlike partnerships, however, REITs cannot pass through losses, only income.

REITs invest in real estate in two ways: as equity owners and as mortgage lenders. Mortgage REITs finance existing or developing properties with first, second or wraparound mortgages. Generally, such mortgages will be "participating"—the REIT earns interest plus a share of increases in rental income and property appreciation. Equity REITs purchase property for cash, or leverage the purchase with mortgage debt. As leverage increases, investors trade cash flow for upside potential from property appreciation because debt service payments reduce cash distributions.

A key attraction of REITs as a vehicle for real estate investment is liquidity. REITs are not marketed on an open-end basis, like mutual funds. So when the offering closes, designated dealers or stock exchange specialists begin making a market in the shares. Investors can add to their holdings or liquidate part of their position by merely calling a stockbroker. The value of the shares is what the market is paying for them. Satisfactory markets are generally unavailable in limited partnership investments.

ADVANTAGES OF FREITs OVER REITs

Originally, all REITs were "perpetual." Proceeds from property sales or loan repayments were reinvested by the REIT. However, the popularity of limited partnerships and the recognition that REIT shares were often valued at a significant discount from the underlying value of their real estate portfolio led to the creation of finite-life REITs—FREITs. In FREITs, proceeds from property sales or mortgage repayments are distributed to investors. So, over time the trust "self-liquidates."

The liquidating feature gives FREITs two advantages over their perpetual-life counterparts. Market values are more reflective of underlying asset values, and share prices are less volatile. Shares of perpetual REITs, like many closed-end investment trusts, are often priced at a substantial discount from the underlying value of the assets. In effect, the REIT share is like a perpetual bond in which principal is never returned. Current cash yield relative to prevailing interest rates paid by alternative income securities determines value. So, if you sell your holdings in a perpetual REIT, you may not get as much for them as they'd be worth were the trust to liquidate.

In contrast, FREIT share prices track underlying asset values more closely, and market fluctuations in share price are less of a problem for FREITs than for perpetual REITs. That's because FREIT valuations rely less heavily on cash flow to determine market value, creating less "interest rate" risk. The reason: The imminence of realized gains from real estate sales will bolster values for FREITs. As properties are sold, significant capital distributions are made, and estimates of value are confirmed (or corrected). As a result, the market valuation of the FREIT shares moves closer to the projected market value of the trust's assets. If interest rates rise, perpetual REIT share values will tend to fall to keep the current yield competitive with other income securities.

BUYING NEW FREIT ISSUES

Partnerships and FREITs differ in the way they are sold. Partnerships are sold during an offering period of weeks or months, allowing investors time to evaluate them at leisure. FREITs, on the other hand, are sold like new-issue stocks and bonds. While brokerage houses underwriting the FREIT take "indications of interest" over several weeks, the offer may open and close in one day.

Obviously, quick sellouts of FREITs confirm investor desire for the liquidity and real estate economics which FREITs offer. While all real estate holdings should be considered relatively long term, FREITs have one psychological advantage which perhaps should not be underestimated: Investors have a chance to change their minds. In times of uncertainty over the direction of inflation, interest rates and tax laws, this flexibility can be a powerful motivation.

SECTION II

EVALUATING
A PUBLIC OFFERING

CHAPTER 10

THREE KEY AREAS TO INVESTIGATE

Once you've matched a type of real estate partnership to investment objectives and risk tolerance, you are ready to select a specific offering. You should evaluate three aspects of any public partnership investment under consideration: (1) the general partner (sponsor organization); (2) the cost of the offering—i.e., the fees and expenses and the compensation paid to the general partner; and (3) any special features the particular partnership offers.

AREA #1: THE SPONSOR ORGANIZATION

Here are the key factors to investigate about the sponsor organization:

- Investment Philosophy
- Qualifications
- Prior Performance

A first-rate sponsor organization will have investment criteria and an acquisition philosophy clearly articulated. Ask about the portfolio of properties the sponsor is trying to assemble to be sure your investment objectives and risk tolerances are met. Most public offerings are "blind pools" or partially blind—properties are acquired after limited partners invest. So, you don't have an opportunity to evaluate specific properties—only the sponsor's strategy.

Regarding investment criteria and philosophy you need to know:

- Type of Property and Tenants
- Phase of Construction
- Leverage (Borrowing)
- Diversification in the Partnership
- Estimated Cash Flow and Tax Loss
- Acquisition Criteria
- Holding Period

You should judge if the investment philosophy "makes sense." Just view the sponsor's objectives against trends or forces in the marketplace that you can personally identify. You won't necessarily be able to judge the future success of the approach, but you'll gain confidence if it feels right to you. Real estate is such a long-term investment, it's almost impossible to see clearly for the entire holding period. However, it's also strategy intensive. A sponsor with a sound strategy now may be able to adapt to change.

There are scores of different investment situations in real estate. Your best bet is to find a sponsor who has specialized successfully in just a few types of investment opportunities. Don't be the one to finance an apartment buyer's first excursion into acquiring office buildings.

Here are the sponsor qualifications you need to check:

- Number of Employees
- Years in Syndication Business
- Investor Capital Raised In Prior Programs
- Financial Condition
- Standing and Reputation

Major sponsor organizations have several hundred employees or more, have been in the business more than five years, and have raised in excess of $100 million of investor capital. You can get an idea of industry standing and reputation by seeing who are the sponsor's attorneys, accountants, and major participating broker/dealers.

The financial condition of the sponsor is important. Pay particular attention to working capital and lines of credit. Be mindful that the general partner of the partnership you are investing in could be a limited net worth subsidiary of the parent sponsor organization. You want facts about the parent sponsor organization's financial capability.

Obviously, an experienced general partner with a full staff should raise your confidence. Look for a staff with real estate acquisition and management experience. Accountants and lawyers may be qualified in their professions, but you want to know their real estate backgrounds if they are key employees.

Prior performance—how well your sponsor has done for investors—is hard to evaluate. Here are ways to judge:

* Results of Liquidated Partnerships
* Record of Property Sales Versus Cost
* Cash Flow Return on Investment

A few sponsors have liquidated previous partnerships by selling all the property and distributing all the cash. You can evaluate performance by calculating the limited partner's rate of return. Unfortunately, comparatively few partnerships have been liquidated.

Occasionally, appraised values of properties still held are provided in annual reports. Here, you can add the aggregate value of economic benefits received to the value of the remaining assets in the partnership. Compare the total to original investment, and you can see how investors are doing. (Partnerships providing this information are the exception rather than the rule. See Section V: "Evaluating Partnership Progress" for a detailed discussion of how to determine the performance of unliquidated partnerships.)

Sponsors typically publish information on the average annual return for properties sold. Sale proceeds are compared to the original investment in the property, and the percentage appreciation is divided by the length of time the property was held. The result is the so-called "Average Annual Appreciation," a number which greatly exaggerates the real rate of return. You should probably disregard this measure of performance.

You can find performance data in the Prior Performance Tables of any public offering prospectus. These tables show the results of the sale of properties in prior partnerships and how successfully the sponsor has managed properties. (A method for analyzing this data is provided in Chapter 23: "Analyzing and Comparing Sponsor Track Records.")

For real estate partnerships to produce attractive investment returns in the 1980s, property must be managed well. During the late 1970s and early 1980s, simply buying and holding leveraged real estate generally resulted in significant capital gains. The reason: Inflation increased construction costs and property values tremendously. The general expectation is for a lower rate of inflation in the near term. So, managing property to increase value will be essential.

Property management is important because real estate values are a function of net operating income. Good management increases net operating income. Probably the most important single factor you need to know is the sponsor's history of improving net operating income (the amount left over when you subtract operating expenses from rental income) for properties under management. (An in-depth method of analyzing the sponsor organization and prior performance is presented in Section IV: "Evaluating The Sponsor.")

AREA #2: OFFERING TERMS

The cost of the investment (called "offering terms"), the fees and expenses and the compensation paid to the general partners, makes an enormous difference in the rate of return in a real estate partnership investment. Good offering terms won't bail out bad real estate. But, good real estate won't always compensate you fully for investing in a deal with excessive costs.

In public real estate programs, differences in partnership offering terms alone can cause the investor's share of return to vary by 40% or more. To illustrate the importance of partnership offering terms, a "bad" deal must acquire property 20% below the price paid by a "good" deal or increase rents 50% faster (highly unlikely) to make up for bad offering terms.

One measure of fairness of offering terms is how the various fees relate to the North American Securities Administrators Association (NASAA) guidelines. (This group sets standards at the state level for real estate partnership offerings.) NASAA's guidelines set maximum fees sponsors can charge, not minimums.

Here's a summary of NASAA fees: Front-end fees may not exceed 20% to 33% of capital contribution. Sponsors are entitled to competitive property management fees plus 10% of annual property cash flow. On property liquidation, sponsors may receive a 3% real estate commission plus 15% of capital gain after the investor gets the original investment back plus a 6% cumulative annual return.

Another way to judge costs of the investment is to compare fees of different partnerships, but this can be a complex job. The impact of front-end, operational and liquidation fees vary with leverage and property performance. Further, the impact of subordination features (which limit the timing and extent of payments to the general partner) complicates the task of analysis. Fortunately, Robert A. Stanger & Co. has developed computer models to accurately compare and rate the relative attractiveness of public and private real estate partnerships in terms of transaction fees. The public partnership ratings appear regularly in *The Stanger Register*. (See Chapters 12 and 13 for a more complete discussion of offering terms and ratings.)

AREA #3: SPECIAL FEATURES

The final consideration in invesment selection is special features of the particular offering you are reviewing. Key considerations are:

- Specified Properties
- Financial Projections
- Ratings
- Appraisals
- Repurchase Options
- Quality of Investor Reporting

Most public real estate partnerships are offered as so-called "blind pools," with no property investments specified in the prospectus. Here, investors are exercising faith in the ability of management to execute an investment philosophy. The availability of uncommitted funds gives the sponsor of a blind pool financial clout in the marketplace for property acquisitions. But, a specified fund is a good feature. If investments are disclosed and committed for purchase, you can take a look at them and determine whether they make sense. Generally, the more properties that are specified in the prospectus, the easier time you will have judging the quality of the portfolio.

Some partnerships and finite-life real estate investment trusts provide financial projections of properties that are acquired. Here you can run your own rate-of-return analysis and determine whether the property meets your investment objectives and risk criteria.

The offering may have a credit rating (Standard & Poor's, Moody's) or a rating from Robert A. Stanger & Co. The credit rating defines repayment risk in a mortgage loan partnership. The Stanger Offering Terms Rating describes the relative attractiveness of the offering terms for all types of RELPs.

Some partnerships will provide appraisals of properties after a few years. This practice gives you a reasonably good idea of the value of the investment at any point in time. The general partner may take this feature a step further and offer to repurchase limited partner units at a price relative to appraised value. An option to re-sell units is an attractive feature.

Take a look at typical reports to investors in past programs. Do you get a feeling from reading the reports that the sponsor tells investors what's going on? If not, pick another sponsor.

CHAPTER 11

GETTING THE INFORMATION: HOW TO READ A PROSPECTUS

This chapter describes a method for analyzing prospectuses based on the format required of publicly registered offerings. While private placement memoranda do not necessarily follow public formats, the basic principles of analysis are the same.

Your primary source of information for a particular partnership investment is the prospectus—a daunting document that can run over 200 pages. If you have the time (and the courage), read the whole prospectus. Otherwise, you can understand the transaction in just fifteen minutes by reviewing these important but brief sections:

1. The cover and the inside cover page of the prospectus.
2. "Who Should Invest."
3. "Summary of the Partnership."
4. "Prior Performance."
5. The "Investments" subsection of "Investment Objectives."
6. Any section describing a special feature of the offering, usually referred to in "Summary of the Partnership." For example, "Repurchase Program."

Here are the reasons these six sections are required reading for a good understanding of the offering.

- **Cover and Inside Cover Page**—Here you can learn the basics of the transaction and determine if it's the kind of investment opportunity you seek. Explained here are the total size of the offering, minimum investment per unit, general partners, proposed investment, partnership investment policy and objectives, and selling commissions and offering costs. Any special or unique provisions will be described as well as whether or not the partnership is a blind pool.

- **"Who Should Invest"**—This section shows the minimum tests investors must meet to be eligible. These tests, sometimes referred to as "suitability standards," state the minimum net worth and/or taxable income investors must have.

- **"Summary of the Partnership"**—This usually is three to six pages and tells you virtually everything else you need to know. You'll find the partnership's investment objectives, unusual features, tax treatments, liquidation and cash distribution objectives, compensation of the general partner and salient investment characteristics like the use of leverage and the type of property to be acquired. Most of the remaining sections of the prospectus merely amplify or define more carefully the general statements on the cover page and in this section.

- **"Prior Performance"**—You want to invest with a general partner who has a proven record. The "Prior Performance" section shows the general partner's past activities. You will be able to identify his length of experience in business, the number of partnerships sponsored, the amount of capital raised, the total dollar value of properties purchased and sold, the approximate percentage of the total represented by each type of property, and the construction status at the time of purchase. You'll also see information on the economic results of liquidated partnerships. (Chapter 23: "Analyzing And Comparing Sponsor Track Records," shows you how to make sense of the performance tables and run some simple comparisons.)

- **"Investment Objectives And Policies"**—You want to be sure the specific investment objectives of the partnership coincide with the general partner's prior activities and business experience. If the general partner is branching out to new investment areas, beware. New skills take time to acquire even if they are still under the general heading of real estate. The place to check is the "Investments" subsection in "Investment Objectives and Policies." Here you'll find a description of the type of property to be purchased, its status at the time of acquisition, preferred locations and management's methods and operating policies in the acquisition process.

- **Descriptions of Special Features**—Next, look at any section that describes unusual features of the offering. You can identify these features from your reading of the cover pages or "Summary of the Partnership." In the prospectus used as the model for this chapter, the unusual feature was described in "Repurchase Program." The general partner agreed to value limited partnership interests and make a repurchase offer. The method was outlined.

You won't have to read more than about ten pages of the prospectus this way, a real time saver. You'll have an excellent idea of the qualifications of the general partner, the nature of the investment, compensation to the general partner and any unusual or distinctive features. If you like what you've read, it makes sense to read the whole document. If not, send the prospectus to the round file.

THE SEARCH FOR PROBLEMS

Lack of management experience or frequent management turnover are danger signs. So, look next at the "Management" section. The "Affiliates" subsection gives you a clear idea of the variety of activities in which the general partner is involved—a guide to depth of experience. The "Officers and Directors of the General Partner" subsection shows the qualifications and experience of individual members of management.

Pay particular attention to the number and experience level of personnel in the property acquisition department. You want to see a background in real estate rather than in the securities industry or legal and accounting professions. Bear in mind that one efficient, experienced acquisition person can usually buy only three or four properties a year. With this yardstick, you can judge for yourself the level of personnel required based on the scope of the partnership's activities. For individuals involved in key functions in addition to acquisitions (like property management, senior management and accounting), notice the length of service with the sponsor. Continuity of management is important.

The good news is that you don't need to read most of the sections containing the "boiler-plate." ("Boiler-plate" is the legal compliance language that is fairly common to all prospectuses.) For the sake of efficiency and time-saving, skim such sections as "Risk Factors," "Conflicts," and "Federal Income Tax Consequences." Here you should look for variances from boiler-plate. (Obviously this becomes easier to do as you gain experience.) Read these sections in any prospectus. If you've read them once, the second go-through is largely repetitious.

In "Risk Factors" you are looking for subsections unique to the offering. If the partnership is involved in acquiring properties under construction, read that subsection. Look for descriptions of investments the partnership intends to make that you weren't aware of, such as "Senior and Junior Mortgage Loans." A heading entitled "Balloon Payments" would show limitations on mortgage loan indebtedness, rather important for a leveraged deal. Another example might be "Other Obligations of Affiliates of the General Partner." If the general partner has obligations (liabilities) important enough for special mention, read on to see what they are.

"Conflicts of Interest" is usually written to give management wide latitude in operating the company—potentially a mixed blessing. Conflicts in the area of general partner fees for services are amply covered in other sections of the prospectus, so don't bother with them here. However, you should concentrate on any text describing capital transactions with affiliates and related parties. Conflicts in this area are almost impossible to manage in a manner fair to investors. Unless such transactions and related self-dealing practices are prohibited in the language of this section, they are permitted. Caveat emptor.

The main use of "Federal Income Tax Consequences" is for your general education. A thorough reading will tell you exactly how the tax aspects of these transactions work. But, 95% of the language is the same in all prospectuses. The trained eye looks here for new sections not normally included in other prospectuses and also at the matters for which an opinion of tax counsel is provided or an IRS ruling is sought.

Take a brief peek at "Underwriting" to see whether or not the broker/dealer listed on the cover page is affiliated with the general partner. If so, be sure an independent organization has looked at the general partner, the offering memorandum and the economic feasibility of the deal. "Legal Opinion" and "Experts" will give you the names of the attorneys and accountants involved in the transaction—one form of quality check. On "Litigation," the less you find, the better.

"Summary of the Partnership Agreement" contains two important subsections you should read: "Distributions—Profit and Losses" and "Compensation and Other Promotional Benefits of the General Partner." Often the most complete description (outside of the Partnership Agreement itself) of the business terms of the deal can be found here, so it's wise to read for a thorough understanding.

THE FINAL STROKES

"General Partner's Discussion and Analysis of Financial Condition" and "Financial Statements" can be revealing. In many cases, a new entity is formed to be general partner of each partnership, and the financial information reflects a start-up company. Totally uninformative. You'll want to ask about the financial condition of the sponsor if it is not available here.

The "Compensation Table" spells out payments to the general partner and others (usually better defined in "Summary of the Partnership Agreement"). Fees are typically divided as either front-end costs, operating phase fees or liquidation phase fees. Many general partners charge the maximum permissible fees under state securities law requirements. Any reduction, or change, in fees from these levels is usually well highlighted elsewhere in the prospectus.

You want to know what communications investors can expect from the general partner. The requirements of the general partner are spelled out in "Reports to the Limited Partner." Often general partners provide more information than the minimum required in the prospectus, so inquire about these practices.

Before you decide to subscribe, it is wise to read the "Glossary" to be sure your understanding of the terms is consistent with how they are used in the prospectus. Since the "Partnership Agreement" is the document investors sign, you must take responsibility for reading it. If the prospectus was well prepared, this exercise will be pure repetition. Now that you've completed your investigation, the final step is to read the "Subscription Agreements."

CHAPTER 12

PARTNERSHIP OFFERING TERMS: A CRITICAL VARIABLE

Not surprisingly, the most important factor in investment performance of real estate partnerships is property appreciation. But, the fees charged the partnership by the sponsor run a close second. Here are conclusions from our analysis of the impact of fees in public real estate programs:

- Low fees, or investor charges, can allow the limited partner a 40% higher dollar return than high fees, assuming identical property appreciation.

- An overall high level of fees can neutralize significant differences in property appreciation, say the difference between 7% and 10% appreciation per annum.

- A high-fee partnership would have to raise rents up to 50% faster than a low-fee partnership to make up for bad offering terms.

- Adverse offering terms can also neutralize favorable property acquisition prices. For example, the sponsor of a "bad" deal must acquire property 20% below the price paid by a "good" deal to provide the same return to the limited partners.

- The faster property appreciates, the more disadvantageous are high fees.

- Picking real estate programs with low fees maximizes your chance of achieving the best overall economic result.

Of course, you should never select an investment based on fee structure alone. But fees should be "fair." One measure of fairness is how fees relate to the North American Securities Administrators' Association ("NASAA") policies. At the state level, this group helps set standards for transactions. The standards set maximum charges. Sponsors are free to charge less. The NASAA standards and definitions of the three categories of fees are shown in the table below.

FEES IN PUBLIC REAL ESTATE PARTNERSHIPS

Front-End Fees—include sales commissions for the broker/dealer, offering and organization costs and property acquisition fees paid to the general partner and unaffiliated third parties. The NASAA front-end fee standard is 20% of limited partner capital contributions for unleveraged partnerships, 28.1% for 50% leveraged partnerships and 33% for 80% leveraged partnerships. For mortgage loan partnerships, the front-end fee standard is 18% of limited partner capital contributions.

Operational Phase Fees—are typically paid to the general partner from cash flow (earnings) of the real estate as compensation for management of the day-to-day operation of the partnership and the properties. NASAA approves "Property Management Fees" equal to 6% of gross revenues for residential properties and 3% of gross revenues for commercial properties plus a "promotional" interest of 10% of annual cash flow (if the Liquidation Phase Fee from net proceeds, explained below, is limited to 15%).

Liquidation Phase Fees—are payable to the general partner upon sale or refinancing of the properties. These fees consist of a real estate commission and a percentage of the net proceeds from the sale or refinancing of the property. Normally, these fees are subordinated (not paid to the general partner) until the return of the limited partner's investment, plus a minimum return. NASAA approves a real estate commission to the sponsor not to exceed 3% of the gross sales price. The promotional or incentive fee is limited to 15% (if the sponsor also received 10% of annual cash flow) or 25% otherwise. The real estate commission and the appreciation percentage are "subordinated" to return of limited partner capital plus a minimum return of 6% per annum on initial capital reduced by periodic cash distributions.

Another way to judge the "fairness" of offering terms is to compare fees of different partnerships. But, front-end, operational and liquidation fees, and subordination provisions (which limit the timing and extent of payments to the general partner) are interdependent. Sorting out the investment implications of the terms is like separating the yoke from a scrambled egg.

Here are some rough guidelines you can use. Differences in front-end fees among publicly registered programs impact the limited partner's rate of return more than twice as much as any other component in deal structure. Variations in operational fees (especially in unleveraged programs) are of second highest importance. Differences in liquidation fees are the third most important factor. But as leverage increases, liquidation fees become more important relative to operational fees.

When investing in a real estate program with relatively high liquidation fees or relatively low leverage, look closely at the program's provisions for "cumulative preferred return" to the limited partner. ("Cumulative preferred return" refers to the limited partners' receipt of initial investment plus a minimum annual return on investment before the general partner receives compensation.) NASAA's minimum "subordination" provisions, requiring 6% return per annum on unreturned capital, protect limited partners if there's little property appreciation but don't matter much when appreciation is significant. The reason: Most properties will almost certainly pay out close to a 6% return over a ten-year period anyway. But, high cumulative preferred return increases the investor's share of partnership earnings considerably.

STANDARD ANALYTICAL TOOL

Until recently, the lack of standards for comparing partnership fee structures made it difficult for you to determine whether a sponsor offered "competitive" terms. Now, Robert A. Stanger & Co. has developed a system for comparing apples to oranges to peaches—a fitting analogy for describing the various offering terms prevalent today. This system provides a standard for accurate comparisons—Stanger's Offering Terms Ratings, published monthly in *The Stanger Register*. The derivation and application of these ratings are described in the next chapter.

CHAPTER 13

RATING PARTNERSHIP OFFERING TERMS

Partnership offering terms are only one element in analyzing a real estate syndication. But as you've seen in the previous chapter, they are a vital element. Sound property acquisition and good management can increase the size of the investment pie. Leverage (borrowing to acquire properties) and appreciation are important too. But in public programs, differences in partnership offering terms alone can cause the investor's share of the pie to vary by 30% or more—a very big slice. The difference in private placement transactions is considerably greater.

Offering terms are particularly important in evaluating public partnerships because they are about the only thing you have to go on. The reason: Track record information is incomplete, sometimes misleading and often compiled differently by each sponsor. Regrettably, few sponsors provide appraised values for older partnerships. Property sales statistics are inadequate because less than 10% of the real estate syndication industry's properties have been sold. Knowing what the other 90% is worth would help you judge performance, but you are rarely given the information.

In any event, most public partnerships are totally "blind" (no property purchases are designated in the prospectus) or only partially specified on closing. Even if the properties are identified, few investors or advisors are up to the task of evaluating property acquisitions. If accountants can't comprehend the real estate syndication industry's partnership financial reporting, what chance does a layman have?

Here's the good news: Offering terms are one factor you can evaluate with certainty **before** making an investment. The prospectus spells out the fees and general partner compensation in considerable detail.

The bad news: Evaluating deal terms is extremely time-consuming and complicated, even with the aid of a computer. Front-end, operational and liquidation fees interact complexly as leverage and property performance vary. Subordination features further complicate the task of analysis. To appreciate the difficulty, consider the partnership arrangements shown below (taken from actual publicly registered offerings). Which is better for the investor?

SAMPLE PARTNERSHIP OFFERING TERMS

	Partnership A	Partnership B
Leverage	55%	0%
Front-End Fees	21%	17.2%
Operational Phase Fees	10% of distributable cash subordinated to 6% cumulative annual return on adjusted capital to limited partners.	5% of distributable cash from operations.
Liquidation Phase Fees	15% of sale proceeds after return of limited partner capital plus 6% cumulative annual return. Commission of 3% of sales price subject to the same subordination.	1% of sale proceeds until limited partner return of capital plus 12% cumulative annual return; thereafter 20%. Commission of 3% of sales price subject to the same subordination.

See the problem? (Incidentally, Partnership A has the most favorable offering terms, but it's certainly not apparent from casual inspection.)

Robert A. Stanger & Co. has developed a rating system to accurately reflect the impact of complex fee structures on investors' potential return. This system gives you a true picture of the relative attractiveness of offering terms.

Robert A. Stanger & Co. rates all publicly registered real estate partnerships on the market. (Private placements are also rated.) The method uses computer analysis of program fee structures, financing chracteristics, property investment models and investor tax brackets—30 variables in all. While the exact formulas are proprietary, essentially, the investor's after-tax, time-valued return from the partnership is compared with the return produced by the same partnership with no syndication costs or fees. The rating is a single figure which is an average of six models representing a distribution of property performance outcomes. The higher the rating, the better the deal for investors.

With this method, the wide variety of programs on the market today are truly comparable. Of course, property performance is impossible to predict. Stanger's Offering Terms Rating does not predict the real return investors will earn in the investment. Rather, the rating system compares partnership returns achievable if property performance were the same.

Each Stanger Offering Terms Rating is composed of a numerical value and a corresponding letter rating based on the following scale:

RATING SCALE

AAA+	86.5 or higher
AAA	82.0 – 86.4
AA+	77.5 – 81.9
AA	73.0 – 77.4
A+	68.5 – 72.9
A	64.0 – 68.4
BBB	63.9 or lower

"A" rated offerings generally have more favorable terms than required by North American Securities Administrators Association guidelines for maximum compensation to general partners. "BBB" rated offerings may be considered below investment grade.

Among publicly registered programs, ratings typically range from BBB to AAA+. What does that mean to you? Investment return can vary up to 41% due solely to the difference in offering

97

terms. In other words, if two partnerships with high (AAA+) and low (BBB) Stanger's Offering Terms Ratings were equally successful in acquiring, managing and selling properties, the total return per $10,000 invested could vary from $23,000 to $32,000.

The table on the next page illustrates the impact of offering terms on investment return for a hypothetical leveraged real estate partnership. You can use this table to better understand and quantify the potential benefit of selecting investments with favorable ratings. Although the absolute level of return will vary between typical leveraged, unleveraged and mortgage loan real estate partnerships, you can use the numerical value associated with Stanger's Offering Terms Rating to measure the limited partners' share (percentage) of total return to the partnership. For example, investors get 86.5% of the total time-valued return in the AAA+ rated program versus 58.8% of the total return in the BBB rated program.

To use Stanger's Offering Terms Rating effectively, you should first choose the type of real estate partnership investment which best fits your financial goals and tolerance for risk using Stanger's Guide To Real Estate Partnership Selection shown in Chapter 3. Next, use Stanger's Offering Terms Rating to screen offerings on the market today and weed out those with unacceptable terms. Finally, review the sponsor to select superior organizations. (You can find profiles of every program currently on the market, including Stanger's Offering Terms Ratings and Risk Ratings, each month in *The Stanger Register.*)

POTENTIAL IMPACT OF OFFERING TERMS ON RETURN
PER $10,000 INVESTED
(Based on Hypothetical Leveraged Real Estate Partnership Investment)

Rating*		Total Return	% Increase In Return Over BBB Rated Partnership
AAA+	(86.5)	$32,292	41.0%
AAA	(82.0)	30,543	33.4%
AA+	(77.5)	29,069	26.9%
AA	(73.0)	27,135	18.5%
A+	(68.5)	25,835	12.8%
BBB	(58.8)	22,898	0.0%
Difference in Total Return Between BBB Rated and AAA+ Rated Partnerships		$ 9,394	41.0%

NOTES: Table shows the potential increase in return to limited partners as partnership offering terms become more favorable. The analysis assumes partnership properties are purchased and sold for ten times net operating income and held for ten years. Operating expenses are 37% of gross revenues in the first year. Rents and expenses escalate 6% annually. Properties are financed with a 30-year, 12.5% fully amortizing mortgage for 65% of the purchase price. The seven structures analyzed (AAA+, AAA, AA+, AA, A+, A, BBB) are illustrative of public programs on the market today.

* Numerical ratings used in the analysis are indicated in parenthesis. Generally, these numerical values define the low range of the rating category. The numerical rating values represent the investor's percentage share of time-valued total return to the partnership.

SECTION III

EVALUATING
A PRIVATE PLACEMENT

CHAPTER 14

ANALYZING A PRIVATE PLACEMENT

Real estate private placements can be analyzed logically, but regrettably, there are no absolutes. The right way to look at a transaction is to look at the whole cloth. You can't isolate specific terms or features. Whether or not the deal is for you depends on the quality and nature of the real estate you want and your investment objectives.

In private placements, you must choose between economics (cash flow and capital gains) or tax loss—you can't have both. (See Chapter 19: "Choose Your Benefit: Syndication Trilogy" for a detailed illustration of the trade-off.) One easy way to understand this statement is to think about leverage. The more leverage, the greater the tax deductions per dollar of equity capital. But, cash flow decreases with leverage because debt service is higher.

All real estate transactions have flaws. It's always easier to turn down a deal than invest in it. Ultimately, you will develop your own set of "deal breakers." Investment decisions should start with an analysis of the property—the asset quality and value. Then, look at the qualifications of the people involved, the general partner and the sponsor organization (syndicator). Next, examine the deal terms, program feasibility and relative value.

ASSET QUALITY

Everyone says it about real estate—what's important is location, location, location. In theory, there is only one "best" location in town for any type of property. It's called the "one hundred percent corner." The best location for one type of property is not necessarily the best location for another type of property. Think of the difference in prime location between a garden apartment and a department store. Location is clearly one test of asset quality.

The physical condition of the property is also important. How old is it? Is maintenance up to date or has it been deferred? Are any significant property improvements required? What is the construction standard? Is the space modern? How does the property compare with recently built competitive space? Inspection reports and engineering studies provide useful information.

One way to get a handle on both location and physical condition is to look at a comparable building in the town in which you live. By visiting a nearby property that's similar, you can get an excellent feel for the relative quality of the property in the partnership. Have the general partner point one out for you.

Asset quality is affected by supply and demand. You should get an idea of the amount of square feet of comparable space in the market and an estimate of the new space under construction (supply). Take a look at the occupancy rate for similar space and, importantly, the absorption rate—the number of incremental square feet of newly available space rented per annum (demand). These facts will give you an idea about market growth, the current status of the market and supply/demand on a longer term basis. Compare these results to current occupancy in the property being purchased and the occupancy level required to break even (i.e., produce a positive cash flow after operating expenses and debt service).

The specific property being bought must be "marketable" to tenants. An apartment project consisting solely of one-bedroom units may not make sense in a family market. Office space with attached warehouse areas needs tenants who are in manufacturing or distribution. Is this type of tenant available?

Asset quality is also defined in economic terms. Terms of tenant leases can radically affect the economics of a property. How long are the leases? What are the rents? Who are the tenants? How do rents stack up compared to the "going rate" in the market?

Another economic factor is financing terms. Financing can make or break a deal. Through early loan maturities or high lender participations in profits, risk may increase and the equity value of the property can be eroded.

VALUE

All economic decisions, including real estate investments, are made on the same basis—value. Value is a combination of quality and price. To judge price, studying "comparable" property transactions is extremely important. "Comparables" are similar properties in terms of asset quality. See what price they change hands for in the market. Compare the prices with the price the partnership is paying.

Price can be compared many ways—per square foot, per apartment unit, per acre, on the basis of "gross rent multiplier" (purchase price divided by gross rental income) and "capitalization rate" (net operating income divided by the purchase price). These measures are static, a snapshot at a point in time. Property is really worth the income generated over its life. You can calculate a rate of return from a moving picture, a financial projection on the property. Often, investment decisions are based on this way of looking at price. (Chapter 15 explains how to use a variety of property valuation tools.)

Value can be influenced by the financing terms offered by the seller. Suppose two properties change hands at the same price— one is bought for all cash; the other is paid for over five years. You can afford to pay more for the second one because you don't have to come up with the entire purchase price today.

Value can be affected by general partner guarantees. If the current market for renting the property is questionable, the general partner may be willing to cover the risk of vacancy. The general partner will lease the property back or hold some of the purchase price in escrow to help the partnership pay debt service when there are cash flow deficiencies.

SPONSOR'S QUALIFICATIONS

The most important qualification of syndication organizations is personnel. The best background is a real estate background—not law, accounting or stock brokerage. The best sign of a well-run organization is the stability and length of service of personnel in the upper ranks. The longer the syndication company has been in business, the better. Also, you need an organization capable of performing a full range of services.

A real estate organization sizeable enough to be a good syndicator has many operating divisions. The acquisition department is probably the most important. The involvement of senior management in the buying process is a good sign. Financial and operational criteria should be established and followed in the acquisition procedure. The acquisition team should visit sites of properties acquired, prepare pro forma financial statements, directly analyze rents and expenses of comparable properties, and involve both the management and legal departments in the acquisition process. Direct contact with developers may result in better acquisition prices than if the syndicator buys through real estate brokers.

Property management is the second most important function. During the term of ownership the syndicator will make a myriad of decisions concerning rent levels, repair and maintenance, property taxes and financing. The most important decision is when and how to sell the property.

Supervising property management of third-party agents requires an information processing capability to measure performance closely. Except for luck or market circumstances, improving the value of the property will be a function of the quality of property management. In general, you have to increase the net operating income to increase the value.

Other departments required to run a syndication operation are the legal department, investment record-keeping and reporting, and accounting and administration. In this financially complicated world, a key ingredient is a senior financial officer who has lending or investment banking experience.

Good sponsors maintain budgets and projections. Variances are noted monthly. Senior management is involved in analyzing performance and making corrections.

One method of evaluating the qualifications of the sponsor is to evaluate prior performance. At the property management level, look for a history of increasing rents faster than expenses so that net operating income (before debt service) expands. You should look at annual operating statements of a significant portion of all recent acquisitions. Be sure the figures you look at only include rental income and operating expenses. Don't mix in other partnership income such as interest.

The financial condition of the sponsor is an important consideration in an investment decision. The sponsor should remain financially stable during the investment period. A private placement purchased from a known, reputable real estate company probably will serve you best. Normally, the net worth of the sponsor will not be disclosed in the offering materials— just the net worth of the general partner. Often, the general partner is a newly formed, limited-net-worth subsidiary of the sponsor. Don't take the sponsor's net worth for granted. Ask.

(Section IV provides an in-depth method for evaluating public and private sponsor organizations.)

OFFERING TERMS

Fees in private placements can be confusing. Fees paid to the seller of the property should not be included in your analysis of a deal. All payments to the seller of the property are part of the purchase price, and you should assume they were negotiated at arms length. But, be aware of one of the fraudulent tricks in private placements—the multiple transfer of property prior to syndication. Here, just the last property sale is described in the offering memorandum. But, there may have been other recent transfers marking up the price of the property substantially.

The fees you should examine are paid to the syndicator, or the broker/dealer, in the transaction. Identifying all "fees" can be difficult. Fees in private placements, as in public offerings, are at the front-end, during the operational phase and during the liquidation phase. But, syndicators also receive interests in property such as leasebacks, land "carve-outs," deferred compensation arrangements, retained mortgages, etc. Here are some examples:

- **Wraparound Mortgage**—The wraparound mortgage (the "wrap") is one way syndicators are compensated in private placements. The mortgage is called a wraparound because the wrap lender (syndicator) agrees to pay off the original mortgage (the "first") on the property. The principal amount of the wrap in excess of the principal amount of the first mortgage outstanding is the syndicator's "equity" in the wrap, the amount of his initial compensation.

- **Building-Equity Wrap**—The syndicator can build "equity" in a wrap (even if the principal amount remains the same as the first mortgage) by charging a higher rate of interest on the wrap. The increased debt service payments compensate the syndicator. The higher interest rate will reduce the investor's annual cash flow. If the syndicator converts the mortgage constant (total annual debt service payment) to an "interest only" payment, this will leave a larger principal balance on the wrap than on the first at maturity (sometimes called a "balloon").

- **Accrued Interest Wrap**—Another favored use of wraps is to charge interest at a rate higher than the property can pay. Unpaid amounts are due when the wrap matures or the property is sold or refinanced. This method can double the original principal balance of the mortgage over, say, a twelve-year period. The Tax Reform Act of 1984 imposed new rules which limit this technique.

These wrap variations increase tax losses in a private placement. That's o.k. But remember, mortgage payments and mortgage payoff occur before investors collect any cash flow from the property or from the sale of the property. These arrangements give the syndicator a priority of interest in cash flow and appreciation before the limited partners.

- **Land Carve-Outs**—Sometimes syndicators acquire both the land and the building but only convey the building to the partnership. Investors usually pay for both, but the syndicator ends up owning the land. These land carve-outs can appear favorable to the partnership. Land is not depreciable. Investors are left with a higher percentage of depreciable assets—a tax advantage. Land rent will generally be low (looking like a bargain) in relation to land value, essentially because the syndicator has no cost in the land. This practice makes comparing the purchase price paid by the partnership with the price of other properties more difficult because their sale price will usually include the land. Also, land leases often call for a percentage of proceeds of sale to be paid as additional rent.

- **Deferred Fees**—Another area of syndicator compensation is charging service fees which are not paid in cash but accrue, payable when the property is sold or refinanced. A popular item here is called the deferred management fee. The unpaid amounts compound and can build to a very substantial sum in ten or twelve years. (The Tax Reform Act of 1984 severely curtails the use of this device.)

As a rule of thumb, fees to the syndicator from the proceeds of the offering should not exceed 20% to 25% of the investor's capital contribution. A better number is 15%. The level of fees paid from your capital contribution will vary depending on other compensation to the general partner from property operations and sale.

Be sure there is a reserve for contingency of 10% to 15% of your capital contribution. Unforeseen needs for cash constantly arise when you own a property.

To calculate the overall fairness of fees, you can use an investment model. One method is to assume the property is purchased as stated in the offering memorandum and then operated according to the pro forma financial projection in the offering memorandum. In other words, look at the deal as if the property were purchased outright, not in a syndication. When the property is sold in the projection, calculate the rate of return on the syndicator's cost.

Then, calculate the return net to the limited partner assuming all the fees and charges in the syndication apply. The return to the limited partner in the syndication should be at least 70% of the return on the property without the syndication.

Sounds straightforward? It isn't. Interest on your partnership capital contributions, deferred and accrued syndicator fees, fees paid to sellers and property financing terms must be sorted out before you turn on your calculator. (We'll show you the ropes in Chapters 16 and 17.)

You can judge the deal's fairness an easier way. Robert A. Stanger & Co. has devised an offering terms rating system for private placements similar to the public system described in Chapter 13. Ask the sponsor how his partnership stacks up based on Stanger's Private Placement Offering Terms Rating.

PROGRAM FEASIBILITY

Can the projections be met? Even financial projections attested to by a prominent CPA firm aren't guaranteed. One thing is certain: The actual performance of the property will be different than the projections.

Variances between projections and reality are usually caused by these factors: the assumption about the length of the rent-up period (if the property is new or under-occupied at the time of purchase); when positive cash flow appears, especially in highly leveraged transactions; and the sale price assumptions, a factor both of the assumed capitalization rate on sale and the appreciation assumptions in the financial projections. You should require special justification when appreciation is above 6% in projections.

Can the partnership's investment objectives be met? Here's some news for you: The odds of achieving significant appreciation in a transaction are remote if the projections show a tax loss of 2-to-1 or more during pay-in. In such a transaction, the odds are also remote of receiving any significant cash flow during the period of ownership. Private placements which are net leases will generally provide little residual value net of the tax cost on sale.

After holding a leveraged partnership for six to ten years, "the tax lines cross." Here, taxable income exceeds cash flow, producing so-called "phantom income." Usually when the tax lines cross in net leases and other tax-oriented real estate transactions, investors don't want to continue paying tax on phantom income until the mortgage is repaid. The most sensible economic decision is usually to sell the property. Equity value at the time of sale will depend on the tax rules prevailing then for the buyer. If the new buyer can structure the transaction to create the same amount of tax losses the original partnership earned, investors will get their money back. If not, he'll pay less than the partnership paid for the investment.

The tax consequences of the transaction are also critical. You need an accountant on your side to assess the risks. The real estate private placement industry has not suffered much at the hands of the IRS. Very few instances are reported of reductions in tax benefits when real estate partnerships are audited. This fact is amazing because tax assumptions used by syndicators are often aggressive. But, the Tax Reform Act of 1984 now requires all "tax shelters" (investments with cumulative deductions exceeding 2-to-1 in any of the first five years) to register with the IRS. Taxpayers must indicate these registration numbers on their returns. The result: The risk of audit is substantially higher and accurate assessment of tax risk is more important than ever.

RELATIVE VALUE

Two ways to measure relative value are: comparing the transaction you are looking at with other similar deals, and comparing it with other types of partnerships available for investment. In other words, how do subsidized housing deals compare to each other, and how do subsidized housing deals compare to office buildings or, for that matter, oil income programs?

When comparing partnerships purchasing similar types of property, you can break down the analysis into components. One component of return is the tax benefits. What are the tax losses during pay-in and over the holding period? Do tax losses come from depreciation, operating losses, leverage or fees?

The other component of return is the economic, or cash, benefits of the investment. What cash distributions can investors expect? Will the asset appreciate in value? Predominantly tax-oriented transactions tend to produce little gain in value during the holding period. Transactions economically oriented can multiply your investment value three or four times, even with reasonably conservative appreciation assumptions.

One way to analyze economic value is to compare the expected value when tax benefits run out to the cost of the investment. Another method is to discount all the benefits from the investment (tax and economic) to present value, then compare this present value with the cost of the investment. Another method is to determine the length of time required to recover your investment after tax—the so-called pay-back period.

Time-valued rates of return are calculated by various methods. The internal rate of return (IRR) is most often used. Here, you discount future pay-ins to present value at a "safe rate" (after-tax bond rate) to calculate the investment amount. The rate that discounts the benefits (tax savings, cash flow and terminal value—all after tax) to the investment amount is the after-tax internal rate of return. (Many advisors prefer the "adjusted rate of return," or the "modified internal rate of return.") If you rely on mathematical calculations, decide on the one you favor and evaluate all investments consistently.

(Chapter 20: "Four Ways To Measure Investment Value" gives you a detailed comparison of today's most widely used rate-of-return measures.)

One problem when comparing different investments using rate-of-return analysis is the probability of achieving the projected result. For instance, a single-project research and development partnership could show a 38% internal rate of return. But, the odds of success are one in nine. Buying "up and built" office buildings may show a 14% internal rate of return. But, the odds of success are almost one out of one. You should adjust quantitative return measures to reflect the probability of success.

CHAPTER 15

GAUGING PROPERTY VALUE

Because private placements generally invest in a single, specified property (versus an unspecified diversified portfolio in public partnerships), it's vital to assess the real estate's current value and economic potential. "Original Sin" in a real estate deal is overpaying badly for the asset. Usually the eyes are glazed over by the prospect of large tax losses per dollar of investment, especially in private placements. Except for subsidized housing, rehabilitation and net leases, large tax losses are not available in real estate deals unless investors overpay for the asset or take a very aggressive tax posture.

Independent property appraisals and engineering reports are useful, but they may not always be available. Sometimes you can get this information from the lending institution (such as a bank or savings and loan) which is providing a permanent mortgage on the property. In any case, financial intermediaries and investors often are not qualified to make detailed property evaluations themselves. However, you can use a few standard real estate valuation tools to get a good feel for the property's value. By comparing these measures to those prevailing in local markets you can separate viable deals from the outrageous and pinpoint the right questions to ask the sponsor.

CAPITALIZATION RATE

The "free-and-clear" capitalization rate is an easy and meaningful measure of real estate value—the first place to start when looking at the math of a real estate syndication. Understand this simple tool, and you'll be able to compare properties in syndications.

The free-and-clear cap rate measures the current return on the property before debt payments—the net operating income (rents less operating expenses) divided by the purchase price. In stock market terms, it's the current earnings yield. The higher the capitalization rate ("cap rate"), the higher the current yield on purchase price or the lower the acquisition price in relation to property cash flow.

To calculate the cap rate, look at the financial projection ("pro forma") on the property—the table that shows rents and operating expenses (utilities, taxes, maintenance, etc.). Typically, the pro forma financial presentation subtracts operating expenses from rents to show net operating income ("NOI") before debt service (interest and principal payments on the mortgage). NOI represents the cash earnings generated by the property. These earnings are the source of value for investment real estate. So, you should focus on projected NOI.

To calculate the free-and-clear cap rate, divide the NOI by the purchase price. Typical free-and-clear cap rates are in the 8% to 10% range for most types of property. ("Free-and-clear" is a real estate term referring to a property not subject to mortgage debt. So, the free-and-clear cap rate is calculated on NOI, which is earnings assuming there is no debt on the property.)

You can also calculate an "equity" cap rate, the current earnings yield on cash investment ("equity"), rather than on the total property purchase price (which includes the mortgage debt on the property as well). Subtract debt service from NOI. The result is "net cash flow" ("NCF"). Divide NCF by the equity investment, and you have the equity cap rate.

Here's an example. Assume you buy a $10 million property for $2.5 million in cash and a $7.5 million mortgage (see Table I). The free-and-clear cap rate is the property's NOI of $1.0

million divided by $10 million, or 10%. The equity cap rate is the net cash flow of $100,000 divided by $2.5 million, or 4%.

TABLE I

CAP RATE CALCULATIONS

Property Purchase Price	$10,000,000
Cash Investment (Equity)	$ 2,500,000
Mortgage	$ 7,500,000
Rents	$ 1,500,000
Less: Operating Expenses	− 500,000
Net Operating Income (NOI)	$ 1,000,000
Free-and-Clear Cap Rate	**10%**
(NOI ÷ Property Purchase Price)	
Less: Debt Service	− 900,000
Net Cash Flow (NCF)	$ 100,000
Equity Cap Rate	**4%**
(NCF ÷ Cash Investment)	

The stability of free-and-clear cap rates makes them better measures of property values than equity cap rates. Suppose an aggressive buyer is willing to pay $11.1 million for the property in our example. The free-and-clear cap rate drops to 9% ($1 million of NOI divided by $11.1 million purchase price). Probably the amount you can borrow will remain the same because the earnings of the property (the amount available for mortgage payments) remain the same. So, to come up with $11.1 million, you'll need $3.6 million in cash. The equity cap rate is now 2.8% ($100,000 divided by $3.6 million). In our example a 10% free-and-clear cap rate fluctuation (from 10% to 9%) causes a 30% drop in the equity cap rate (from 4% to 2.8%) due to the leverage of mortgage debt.

When the current operating statement on the property is not indicative of future results, you can use the "stabilized cap rate" to judge value. For instance, what if you agree to buy a building still under construction, or one where current rents are very low by comparison with going rents in the market? Here, you estimate the year either the property will be finished with all tenants moved in, or the leases will be renegotiated to higher market levels (the "stabilized" year). Normally you would not go out more than a few years from the current date. At this point

117

you expect the property's income statement to remain "stable," to grow only with inflation or with long-term changes in supply and demand.

Looking at the building's income statement for the stabilized year, you calculate the free-and-clear cap rate. Remember, since projections and the uncertainty of time are involved, you'll want to see higher cap rates on the stabilized NOI than prevail in the current market. But, this process lets you use the cap rate concept for nearly any property purchase.

Free-and-clear cap rates can vary somewhat predictably by property type. Rather than representing better or worse bargains, the range of cap rates represents the intrinsic value or risk in different types of property based on the financial quality of the tenant and the length of the lease. The lowest cap rates (highest property values relative to current earnings) are generally found in big shopping centers. Then come office buildings, apartments, strip centers, and hotels in order of rising cap rates.

Caution: The cap rate is a snapshot of the property's earnings at a particular point in time, only part of the story. The amount and terms of financing, future earnings of the property and the ultimate sale price of the property will give the rest of the story and determine the actual rate of return on investment. These factors may change the cap rate that you consider represents a fair purchase price going in. The more earnings growth you expect, or the more favorable the financing, the lower the cap rate you might settle for at time of purchase.

But absent these factors, cap rates are an important indication of potential economic performance. To illustrate the importance of a higher cap rate on purchased property—for every .5% increase in cap rate at purchase, the investor's after-tax internal rate of return increases one full percentage point in the typical leveraged real estate deal. Table II on the next page shows after-tax internal rates of return as acquisition cap rates rise for leveraged, unleveraged and participating mortgage loan partnerships.

TABLE II
IMPACT OF CAP RATES ON
LIMITED PARTNER AFTER-TAX IRRs

Acquisition Cap Rate	Real Estate Equity Partnership		Participating Mortgage Loan Partnership
	Leveraged	Unleveraged	
8.0%	9.5%	9.0%	11.1%
8.5%	10.5%	9.6%	11.4%
9.0%	11.6%	10.4%	11.6%
9.5%	12.6%	11.1%	11.9%
10.0%	13.6%	11.8%	12.1%

Note: Table assumes a 6% annual appreciation rate. The leveraged scenario assumes mortgage borrowing equal to 65% of property purchase price.

GROSS RENT MULTIPLIER

Some real estate professionals use the gross rent multiplier ("GRM") as a rough guide to property value. GRM is simply property purchase price divided by gross rental income (i.e., total rental income before any deductions for operating expenses and debt service). Typical gross rent multipliers range from 6 to 8 for most types of property. The lower the gross rent multiplier, the more favorable the acquisition price of the property.

GRM's are not as accurate as cap rates since the GRM calculation ignores differences in operating expenses. (See Table III below.) Two properties with identical gross rents may produce substantially different current earnings (NOI). Investors should pay for earnings after expenses, so GRMs can be deceiving. Table IV on the next page illustrates the point. Based on GRM, Property #2 appears the best buy. Rental income is

TABLE III
GROSS RENT MULTIPLIER CALCULATION

Property Purchase Price	$10,000,000
Gross Rents	$ 1,500,000
Less: Operating Expenses	− 500,000
Net Operating Income	$ 1,000,000
Gross Rent Multiplier	6.7
(Purchase Price ÷ Gross Rents)	

TABLE IV
GRM VERSUS CAP RATE

	Property #1	Property #2
Property Purchase Price	$10,000,000	$10,000,000
Gross Rents:	$ 1,500,000	$ 1,600,000
Less: Operating Expenses	− 500,000	− 620,000
Net Operating Income	$ 1,000,000	$ 980,000
Gross Rent Multiplier	6.7	6.3
Free-and-Clear Capitalization Rate	10.0%	· 9.8%

$100,000 higher for Property #2, but expenses are $120,000 higher, and current earnings are $20,000 lower. The cap rate accurately reflects the economic advantage of Property #1.

Despite this weakness, GRM can be useful for comparisons with similar properties when information on net operating incomes are not available.

THE PRO FORMA

Financial return methods of property valuation, such as internal rate of return and discounted present value techniques, require projections of property operating results during the entire anticipated holding period; cap rates and GRMs do not. The good news: Measuring value based on the life of the investment allows consideration of future lease turnovers, capital improvements and changes in operating costs and efficiencies. The bad news: Projections become less reliable with each year projected.

While thorough evaluation of projections are best left to appraiser/economists, you can use some simple techniques to identify overly optimistic forecasts. First, compare the assumed annual growth rate of rental income to near-term inflation expectations. If the growth rate is 2% higher than inflation, you should ask for a more conservative scenario.

Watch out for projections where income or NOI in the first year of operations is significantly higher than in the prior year of actual operations. Sometimes such increases can occur when a significant portion of leases are scheduled for renewal in the year of sale. But cranking up NOI in the first year gives the projection a huge leg up and can substantially inflate aggregate return over the life of the investment. When in doubt, ask for justification.

Beware of projections where the rate of annual growth in rents exceeds the growth in expenses. For example, if rents increase at 7% while expenses increase at 5%, you should probably reject the forecast.

Another often overlooked factor in valuation projections is market rent cycles. "Going rents" can fluctuate by 25% or more due solely to building cycles in local markets. Appraisal projections ordinarily take the current market rent level and apply the assumed annual growth rate to determine future lease renewal rates. If rents are at the top in a cyclical market, this process can overstate revenues by more than one-third over a ten-year holding period. You should know where rents stand by looking at long-term trends in the property's market. Recognizing a "top" is probably impossible, but the exercise will help you assess the risk in the projections.

COMPARABLES

Another way to judge value is to compare the price limited partners pay for the property to the prices paid for "comparable" properties (called the "market" approach). Determining which properties are "comparable" involves subjective judgments about location, age, style, amenities, etc. But, again, you'll derive useful benchmarks.

Comparables can be compared based on purchase price per rentable square foot, price per unit (e.g., apartments), gross rent multipliers and capitalization rates. You should probably compare the partnership's property to at least four or five similar properties in the area.

Remember, financing terms can affect property transaction prices significantly. Lower interest rates tend to produce higher purchase prices—in essence, the buyer's equity cap rate remains constant while the free-and-clear cap rate declines. Also, seller financing at below-market rates also tends to increase the contract price of acquisitions. Such financing differences complicate the analysis of comparables. Our recommendation: Press the sponsor to provide an independent professional appraisal.

REPLACEMENT COST

Comparing the price investors pay per square foot to the cost of comparable new construction can be enlightening. Usually, existing properties sell at a 20% to 25% discount, or more, from new construction costs. If the limited partners are buying existing property closer to new construction cost, ask why. Sometimes, such factors as location, current market rents, the nature of tenant leases or favorable financing can explain the apparently high price the partnership is paying. If you are unsure of the explanation you get, you should probably request an appraisal report.

CHAPTER 16

THE PURIFIER:
THE PERFECT SCREEN

The best bargains and the worst deals are both found in real estate private placements. If you're going to try this type of investment, you'd better be able to discern which is which.

Perhaps the best early warning system, or screening technique, for real estate private placements is comparing the operating income of the property with the price investors pay for the partnership. We call it the "Purifier." The Purifier clearly reflects how much investors are paying for the property and indicates whether the transaction is reasonably priced. With only two numbers to compare, you'll save hours of digging through the offering memorandum. That's what an investment screen should be—quick, accurate and useful.

Here's the Purifier in a nutshell: Divide the property's net operating income before debt service (so-called "free-and-clear" net operating income) by the total capitalization of the partnership ("adjusted purchase price"). That's right. The Purifier is a capitalization rate ("cap rate") but figured at the partnership level. In a syndication, you "purify" the property level cap rate by adjusting for all the fees and charges at the partnership level. The reason—you are buying the partnership, not just the property.

The higher the Purifier, the higher the current yield of the transaction and the lower, or cheaper, the price investors are paying for the property. Just like bonds, the higher the yield the lower the price and vice versa. The Purifier is the earnings return, or yield, calculated on the purchase price of the partnership.

Like any quick and dirty technique, the Purifier only tells part of the story. Terms of the financing, the future earnings of the property and tax factors are key elements, too. And, the Purifier doesn't show the cut of the pie between the limited and general partner. But, the point is simple—if the gross purchase price is out of line (low Purifier) it's a bad deal. No amount of creative financing or brilliant structuring is likely to bail you out.

The Purifier is a pretax method of judging value. But, any tax deal won't fly in the long run unless the property purchase price is reasonably right. And, that's exactly what the Purifier will show you.

ALL YOU NEED TO KNOW

The two elements in the Purifier are the net operating income ("NOI") of the property and the total capitalization of the partnership (which is the adjusted purchase price of the property).

You will undoubtedly need to turn to the financial projection, or forecast, in the back of the offering memorandum. To dig out the NOI, find the income statement on the property. Net operating income is rents less operating expenses before deductions for interest, principal, depreciation and partnership items. Take the NOI for the first full year of ownership.

In effect, the total capitalization of the partnership is the amount investors are paying for the property. Why? That's the number the property must be worth on sale for investors to get their money back (ignoring accrued items). The total capitalization of the partnership is the capital contributions ("Equity") added to the total debt ("Debt") of the partnership. The Equity contribution to the partnership is the present value of all cash contributions by the limited partners (and general partner in the unlikely event he contributes cash) including the present value of interest paid on deferred contributions. Add the principal amount of all Debt outstanding. Since Equity can be used to pay off Debt, only look at total Debt outstanding after investors have finished paying in all Equity.

To figure the Purifier divide the property's NOI by the partnership's total capitalization. The Purifier is a current yield—the cap rate of the property figured at the partnership level. The higher the Purifier, or current yield, the better the deal.

CATCH A SYNDICATOR BY THE TOE

The Purifier makes out-of-line syndication fees and markups stand out like Wilt Chamberlin with the seven dwarfs. Roughly speaking, a 10% increase in the purchase price (total partnership capitalization) drops the Purifier 10%. So, high fees will stand out immediately. And, you won't have to go through the agony of trying to find out how investors are being nailed. The Purifier does the work for you. A low Purifier tells you it's a bad deal.

Here's another syndicator sham the Purifier exposes—the tendency to charge the same percentage fee (expressed in terms of the equity) regardless of how much equity is in the deal. Suppose you buy a building for $10 million, with $3 million of equity and a $7 million mortgage. A fair syndication fee is 20% of the equity, or $600,000. That boosts the purchase price 6% to $10.6 million and drops the Purifier from 10% to 9.4%.

Now if you assume an all cash deal with the same **percentage** fee, the purchase price is hoisted to $12 million ($10 million equity plus $2 million fee). In both deals the syndicator's fee is 20% of equity. But, the Purifier drops to 8.3% in the all-equity deal versus 9.4% in the leveraged deal. The low Purifier indicates a bad deal. Way to go, Purifier!

Two lessons—follow the Purifier and be careful when you look at "economic" deals today. One way to be more "economic" is to increase the equity and decrease the debt. Be sure the fees investors pay are proportional to the size of the deal, not the size of the equity.

HOW TO CALCULATE THE PURIFIER

Here's a comparison of two actual private placements. Deal #1 requires $14,836,000 in total capital to purchase an apartment complex generating $800,000 of first-year NOI. The Purifier is 5.4% ($800,000 divided by $14,836,000). Deal #2 requires $10,600,000 in total capital to purchase another apartment complex, also generating $800,000 of first-year NOI. The Purifier is 7.5% ($800,000 divided by $10,600,000). Deal #2's investors are "getting in" at substantially better terms than investors in Deal #1 because the Purifier is much higher, 7.5% versus 5.4%.

HOW TO CALCULATE THE PURIFIER

	Deal #1	Deal #2
Step One: Calculate NOI		
Rents	$ 1,400,000	$ 1,160,000
Less: Expenses	− 600,000	− 360,000
Net Operating Income (NOI)	$ 800,000	$ 800,000
Step Two: Calculate Partnership Capital		
Equity Contribution:		
Year 1	$ 1,288,000	$ 1,070,000
Year 2	1,584,000	1,134,000
Year 3	1,648,000	1,202,000
Year 4	1,712,000	1,274,000
Year 5	1,768,000	1,350,000
TOTAL	$ 8,000,000	$ 6,030,000
Present Value (at 6% discount rate)	$ 7,086,000	$ 5,350,000
Mortgage Balance In Year 6	$ 7,750,000	$ 5,250,000
Total Partnership Capital	$14,836,000	$10,600,000
Step Three: Calculate Purifier		
Divide NOI by Total Partnership Capital	$\dfrac{\$\ 800}{\$\ 14,836} = 5.4\%$	$\dfrac{\$\ 800}{\$\ 10,600} = 7.5\%$

A closer examination of each deal indicates the purchase price paid to the seller of each property was not much different. Deal #1 was a little more expensive. But, the real difference between the two deals is at the partnership level. In Deal #1, the markup and fees are significantly higher. The result: Deal #1 is priced 40% higher than Deal #2. The investment to look into more closely is Deal #2, the one with the highest Purifier.

EXCEPTIONS

Some commonly encountered transactions require care when calculating the Purifier. Often a partnership acquires a partial, or joint venture, interest in property. Where the partnership buys a stated percentage interest across-the-board, say 50%, that's easy to handle. (Across-the-board refers to an identical interest in cash flow, taxable income and gain.) Just be sure you use 50% of the NOI and 50% of the debt to which the property is subject. (You will still have to include 100% of any debt to which only the partnership is subject.)

Where the seller of the property retains an interest that is not across the board, you can still calculate the Purifier. The simplest route is to ignore this circumstance if the interest is minor. Say the seller temporarily retains an interest in the cash flow. Still calculate the Purifier based on 100% of the property-level NOI. Just bear in mind that the Purifier is somewhat overstated because of the seller's cash flow interest. The more complicated approach (but more accurate) is to figure the effective percentage of the net operating income and debt investors are buying. Then calculate the Purifier with these adjusted numbers.

EXCEPTIONS PROVE THE RULE

Some transactions require special consideration when using the Purifier. Be careful when property is:

1. A joint venture, or where the seller retains an interest.
2. Under construction.
3. Subject to leaseback.
4. Currently underperforming (rents significantly lower than market).
5. A special-use facility.
6. Subject to syndicator-provided leverage.

You can screen a new construction, or development, deal with the Purifier. Properties don't generate normalized earning power until a few years after completion of construction. Here, you need to use the NOI in the "stabilized year," the first full year after you expect rent up. (Incidentally, you use stabilized-year debt to figure partnership capitalization, too.)

Often a new construction project is leased back to the seller for a while to insulate the acquiring partnership from property operating losses. As above, go to the stabilized year after the leaseback terminates to find the NOI and use the debt amount in the stabilized year to calculate the Purifier. Since these figures are a few years out and are estimates, you would expect a higher Purifier to balance the risk of uncertainty.

Sometimes, a property with low current income is acquired with the expectation that as leases expire, rents will roll over at higher rates and NOI will increase rapidly. Again, the stabilized-year concept applies. Look at the year you expect income to reflect market rates. But, be reasonable and don't go out more than a couple of years. The reason: The NOI several years out has probably been increased for inflation in the projection and the farther out you go, the more speculation in the numbers.

Special-use facilities (for example, fast food outlets) have value as businesses on top of their value as real estate. Traditional cap rate analysis will usually show a high Purifier. Here, investors are being paid a premium as a participation in the business. So, the return is more uncertain than in a straight real estate investment.

Say you have two properties identical in all respects except one has a mortgage at a lower rate than the other. You are probably thinking the Purifiers would be the same for each property, while the one with the lower rate mortgage is a better deal. You're right about the Purifier. If the purchase price is the same, you are also right about the deal comparison.

But, the property with the lower mortgage rate will probably sell at a somewhat higher price. Why? Because this property will produce higher income after debt service. The Purifier will drop because the price of the property will go up. Favorable leverage may make a deal worth a higher price—you'll accept a deal with a lower Purifier.

Participating (or syndicator-added, accruing interest) debt can make the Purifier higher artificially. The reason: The lender is entitled to some of the NOI, so investors are not earning all of it. Unfortunately, there is no easy way to adjust the Purifier.

No tests or methods of comparison are airtight, and the Purifier is no different.

Remember, the Purifier doesn't predict the rate of return on investment. Over time, you need to calculate the tax benefits, the cash flow and appreciation to figure rate of return. But, the Purifier is an easy method to compare property prices when you are buying into a transaction.

HOW TO USE THE PURIFIER

Cap rates, and hence Purifiers, vary somewhat predictably by property type because of the nature of the tenancy. The higher the financial quality of the tenant and the longer the lease, the lower the cap rate and Purifier and the higher the price for the property. Prices go up for better quality income because the income stream is more predictable. Generally, you earn the lowest Purifier for enclosed shopping malls, and progressively higher Purifiers for office buildings, apartments, strip centers, hotels, mini-warehouses and special use properties.

You should set up a Purifier Pecking Order ("PPO") when comparing deals with different properties. First, there's the property type consideration above. Then, factor other elements in the PPO: Larger properties tend to sell for a lower Purifier (higher price) than small properties; urban lower than suburban; growth areas lower than stable areas; and, prime locations lower than secondary ones.

The general rule: Compare Purifiers for the same kind of property. If one suburban office building has a Purifier of 10% and another office has 5% (a spread we have seen) the message is clear. You are purchasing the 10% Purifier for one-half the price of the 5% one. You shouldn't need any more help picking the better buy!

On the other hand, a hotel at an 11% Purifier is not necessarily a better buy than the suburban office building at 10%. Why? Purifiers for hotels should be higher than Purifiers for office buildings. The Purifier can be high for intrinsic real estate reasons (the PPO), which merely indicates greater risk in the property. The Purifier is only one tool which concentrates on present conditions, not how things may change in value over time.

CHAPTER 17

TWO ACID TESTS: MARKUP AND APPRECIATION TO BREAK EVEN

The Purifier is a quick way to judge the quality of the syndicator's property purchase and the price investors pay to get in on the acquisition. (See Chapter 16.) A Purifier of 8% for an apartment syndication is a "good deal" if local markets value apartments at a 9% cap rate.

You can use two other tests to back up the Purifier: property "markup" at the time of purchase and the property appreciation necessary to break even on sale.

"Markup" is another measure of the fairness of the price investor's pay for the property. Here you compare what the syndicator paid the seller (which usually represents the actual "fair market price") with what investors are paying. The difference is the "markup." How much the property is marked up is obviously important because the cost of a partnership investment should be reasonable in relation to "the market" for similar property. In the process of determining markup, you'll establish a dollar price paid by investors for the property—a useful figure to use when comparing costs per unit or per square foot with going market prices for other properties. "Markup" gives you a single percentage figure indicating the syndicator's front-end compensation relative to the size of the total transaction—more meaningful than looking at compensation relative to equity.

Appreciation to break even tells you how much the partnership needs to sell the property for to return all investor money.

Here, you learn two other important aspects of the deal: (1) the impact of general partner back-end fees, and (2) the "quality" of partnership leverage. Wraparound mortgages, accrued interest mortgages and participating mortgages can all be used to enhance leverage and increase tax losses. But, you "pay up" when properties are sold and the accruals and participations are paid back to lenders. By calculating appreciation to break even, you include the true cost of leverage in your evaluation. The calculation of appreciation necessary to break even also will show whether the investment provides primarily economics or tax benefits.

In the process of making these two calculations, you will have to look closely at the deal—often tricky the way real estate private placements are put together today. But, simplifying the analysis of a deal with these basic tests and the Purifier (see Chapter 16) can save you a lot of time and a small fortune. You can cut out most of the 150 pages or so of a private offering memorandum. If you read a real estate private placement memorandum and can't figure out how much investors are paying for the property and how much appreciation is necessary to recover their cash investment, turn the offer down. Why? The document is too complicated to understand. Need more be said?

In the unregulated private placement market, there are no limits on fees, price markups and general partner compensation. The success or failure of an investment can be a function of what investors are charged. Generally speaking, markups range from 15% to 100% and appreciation necessary to break-even ranges from 20% to 150% for real estate private placements in the market today. Obviously, you should know how to make these calculations.

The concepts are simple but require some math. A few examples of how you handle some of the common elements in deals today will give you the feel of how to look at a transaction you are evaluating.

PURCHASE PRICE

The purchase price of the property from the third-party seller is one place to start an analysis of any real estate deal. The purchase price is the amount of cash the syndicator pays the seller of the property plus the balance remaining unpaid on any mortgages on the property assumed at the time of purchase. If investors are buying a 100% interest in the property and complete the purchase at one time, the cash plus the mortgages equal the purchase price.

Sometimes, in private placements, the syndicator makes what is in effect an installment purchase, paying the cash portion of purchase price to the seller over a period of years. Here, you simply discount each future payment to present value at a realistic after-tax rate, say 8%, to figure the purchase price. (See Figure 1). The facts of the purchase of the property from the seller will be spelled out in the offering memorandum. If not, avoid the deal.

FIGURE 1

	Cash To Seller	First Mortgage Principal	Purchase Price*
Year 1	$1,500	$15,000	$16,500
Year 2	1,500		1,390*
Year 3	1,500		1,290*
Total Purchase Price			**$19,180**

*Present Value at discount rate of 8% per annum.

If the seller takes back a mortgage on the property as well as cash, add the seller's debt amount outstanding only after all installment payments have been made. The investors' cash contribution may be paying off the seller's mortgage. (See Figure 2 on the next page.)

In short, the present value of any amount paid the seller is part of the purchase price. Include both interest and principal payments on debt taken back by the seller. Sometimes gross rents or net cash flow are allocated or paid to the seller. These amounts are additional purchase price as well. Discount any payments to present value. Generally, don't adjust purchase price for cash flow allocations in newly constructed property purchased before rent-up unless the partnership is paying debt service. If the partnership does pay debt service, the present

FIGURE 2

	Cash To Seller	First Mortgage Principal	Seller's Purchase Money Mortgage*	Purchase Price**
Year 1	$1,500	$15,000	$3,000	$16,500
Year 2	$1,500		$1,500	1,390**
Year 3	$1,500		0	1,290**
Total Purchase Price				**$19,180**

*Interest on this mortgage, if any, is additional purchase price.

**Present Value at discount rate of 8% per annum. Only the amount of seller's purchase money mortgage principal outstanding after all installment cash payments to seller have been made is included in Purchase Price. In this example, no purchase money principal is due after year 3.

value of any net profit the seller receives (expected rents less all costs the seller pays) should be added to the purchase price.

The seller may retain a percentage of cash flow and sale or refinancing proceeds. Here, investors are clearly buying less than 100% of the property. Just divide the present value of cash contributions plus the amount of mortgage debt attributable to the partnership by the percentage interest investors are buying in the property to calculate the purchase price for the entire property.

MARKUP

The "adjusted purchase price" is all the cash investors pay into the partnership and all the debt and obligations against the property, or the partnership, when the syndication is complete (i.e., total partnership capitalization). The markup is the difference between what investors pay (adjusted purchase price) and the price the syndicator paid (purchase price). The adjusted purchase price includes all cash amounts paid to all parties to the transaction including the seller, the syndicator, the broker/dealer and third parties for organization expenses, legal fees and even for interest on deferred capital contributions. In short, the cash portion is all the money investors put up, whatever label is attached to it. Just like installment payments to the seller, you discount all these payments back to present value.

In addition to cash, investors are assuming debt (taking the property "subject to" debt). Some of the debt will be the same as the debt on the property when the syndicator bought in. Additional debt (or other obligations to which the property is subject, like fees not currently paid but due eventually) may be added by the syndicator. To figure the adjusted purchase price, combine all the original debt and other obligations added by the syndicator to the present value of the cash investors put in.

In Figure 3, the cash contribution of $8,000 has a present value of $7,150. The property is subject to total debt of $17,500. Investors are paying a total of $24,650 (the adjusted purchase price from Figure 3). The syndicator paid the seller $19,180 (Figure 1). So, the markup is $5,470, or 29%, a fairly reasonable amount in a private placement today (see table below).

FIGURE 3

	Cash To Partnership	First Mortgage Principal	Wraparound Mortgage Principal*	Purchase Price**
Year 1	$2,000	$15,000	$17,500	$19,500
Year 2	$2,000			1,850**
Year 3	$2,000			1,710**
Year 4	$2,000			1,590**
Total Adjusted Purchase Price				**$24,650**

* With a wraparound mortgage, the lender agrees to pay off the first mortgage, so you owe only the balance of the wrap mortgage. In this example, the wrap mortgage is interest only. The balance due remains constant.

** Present Value at discount rate of 8% per annum.

CALCULATION OF MARKUP

Adjusted Purchase Price Paid by LPs	$24,650
Less: Purchase Price Paid By Syndicator	19,180
Markup: Dollar Amount	$ 5,470
Percentage (Dollar Markup Divided By Purchase Price Paid By Syndicator)	28.5%

By the way, you can and should use the adjusted purchase price to compare:

• similar properties;
• cost on a square foot basis;

- gross rent multipliers (adjusted purchase price divided by gross rents);

- Purifiers (net operating income divided by adjusted purchase price);

- rates of return.

APPRECIATION TO BREAK EVEN

Here's how to figure the price at which the property must be sold for investors to break even. The easy way: Usually, a complete private placement memorandum will show all amounts due to others before investors are paid on an assumed date of sale. Add these amounts to all the cash investors put up and that's the bogey—the sale price necessary to break even. Compare this amount with the purchase price to the seller, and you'll see the appreciation needed over the property's initial market value to break even.

Traditionally, mortgages were slowly paid off (amortized) from debt service payments, and this debt reduction increased investor equity in the property (called "equity buildup"). Now, debt service often does not include principal repayments (called "interest-only" debt). Further, as you saw in Chapter 14, syndicators take fees in the form of wraparound loans or deferred payments that can actually increase the balance owed over time. Instead of equity buildup, investors suffer equity meltdown. These arrangements are the principal reasons you must calculate appreciation necessary to break even to see the real cost of the terms of a particular deal.

Figure 4 on the next page illustrates the calculation of appreciation to break even and the impact of financing terms on the break-even amount. In this example, the appreciation necessary to break even is 36% when the property is financed with an interest-only syndicator wrap mortgage versus 12% with a fully amortizing first mortgage.

FIGURE 4
APPRECIATION TO BREAK EVEN
(Sale in Fifteenth Year)

	Property Financing	
	Fully Amortizing $15,000 First Mortgage	Interest Only $17,500 Syndicator Wrap
Mortgage Balance Due On Sale	$12,988	$17,500
Plus: Deferred Fees Due Syndicator	+ 500	+ 500
Original Investment	+ 8,000	+ 8,000
Sale Price To Break Even	$21,488	$26,000
Less: Property Purchase Price	−19,180	−19,180
Appreciation To Break Even:		
Dollar Amount	$ 2,308	$ 6,820
Percentage (Dollar Amount Divided By Property Purchase Price)	12%	36%

*Balance due after fifteen years on a 12-1/2%, fully amortizing 30-year mortgage.

WHAT'S A FAIR DEAL?

Private placements are usually marked up more than public offerings and the appreciation necessary to break even is usually greater. But, the disadvantage of a public offering is that all capital contributions usually are paid in the first year. In the typical private placement, the deferred pay-in of capital over several years serves the purpose of matching more closely capital contributions with tax loss. The net after-tax investment is greatly reduced this way compared to public offerings.

In a typical real estate blind pool public offering, property purchase price is marked up about 15%. And, most operational and liquidation fees are subordinated to the return of the investors' capital. Usually, no additional mortgages or other deferred payment contracts are allowed. So, the appreciation necessary to break even in public deals approximates the original markup in property purchase price.

Since complete payment for a property in a private placement occurs three or four years after pay-in begins, investors should expect to pay more. In effect, they are borrowing the equity short term. In part, the answer to how much more depends on the structure of the transaction and length of time over which property payments are made. A rule of thumb is 30% to 40% more equity pay-in than for a public offering for a three-year pay-in private transaction and 50% more for a five or six-year pay-in.

Increasing the price investors pay for property can increase tax loss deductions because of additional depreciation. Without tax structure gimmickry, losses during pay-in don't exceed $1 per dollar of investment. So, don't be misled. The higher the level of tax loss in relation to investment, the greater the property markup. (See Chapter 19: "Choose Your Benefit: Syndication Trilogy" for a detailed comparison of public and private structuring.)

You should not object to such "tax structuring" per se. But, be sophisticated enough to calculate the economic cost before jumping in. Also, you should know that the IRS has prevailed against taxpayers in cases when too high a property value is assumed in relation to market value, or when property is subject to mortgage indebtedness substantially in excess of real market value. In an adverse ruling, the investor does not own an interest until the property value exceeds the amount of the debt to which the property is subject. Unfortunately, if you don't "own it," you can't depreciate it. So, tax losses would be greatly diminished, and the very motivation for the "tax structured" transaction vanishes.

The good news on the tax side: Private placement transactions today are so complicated that the average Internal Revenue Service agent probably will not understand what is going on. Even though the chance of audit may be significant, investors may not suffer as a result.

Not infrequently, real estate private placements are marked up over 100% and appreciation necessary to break even is even higher. The offset, theoretically, to this high level of markup is that tax losses of two or three times the amount invested are generated. The IRS and Congress are aware of the techniques promoters use to create the hoped-for tax result. This is one area attacked by the Tax Reform Act of 1984. The bottom line: If you buy into a "tax structured" transaction which has been (or will be) outlawed, you've made a terrible investment and probably lost the tax deduction. (See Chapter 4: "Dangers in Tax Deals.")

CHAPTER 18

A QUALITATIVE APPROACH TO FEES

Fees in private placements are not the most important factor in judging a transaction's value. The price the partnership pays for the property is the single most important element in analyzing any real estate private placement transaction. As we showed in Chapter 17, you calculate the property price by discounting to present value all the equity capital (including interest) contributed by the limited partners and adding all the debt to which the property is subject at the conclusion of the pay-in period. That's the adjusted purchase price in dollars. Compare this price to other comparable properties according to the standard measures of real estate value: gross rent multiplier; price per square foot; capitalization rate (net operating income divided by adjusted purchase price—the Purifier); and the sale price of similar properties in the same location.

If the real estate is fairly priced, the importance of fees declines. But, one difficulty with this truism is the inability of most investors and financial intermediaries to determine whether a property price is "fair," or "on the market." Even other real estate professionals would have difficulty second-guessing the acquisition price of a property, because the price alone does not tell the whole story. For instance, a property with low rents and leases expiring in the near term could command a high price in relation to current income.

Fees paid to a syndicator are not all "add-ons." If you bought a property outright, you might well order and pay for an appraisal, you also might have an accountant construct an income statement for the property, hire a lawyer to close the purchase transaction, pay a real estate commission, and conceivably incur cost in refinancing the property. In addition, you might have to travel, investigate the property and negotiate the acquisition. In all cases, you are out both dollars and time.

In a limited partnership investment, the syndicator performs these services or sees they are performed. Reimbursing him is certainly reasonable. In effect, the syndicator enables "passive" investment. The syndicator does the work for investors and provides economies of scale.

As with hiring any financial intermediary or investment advisor, the prime ingredients investors are paying for are experience and good judgment. The syndicator researches real estate markets and properties, analyzes individual transactions, and probably reviews hundreds of acquisitions before selecting one for purchase. The syndicator must negotiate with the seller of the property and put proper financing in place. Investors also pay for judgment concerning leasing, operating and finally disposing of the property.

The syndicator can be a risk manager by negotiating guarantees from the seller or by stepping in himself. As a result, investors can be partially insulated from the cost of renting up the property on time or operating the property at a cash loss.

In syndications, investors normally pay more than if they acquired the property outright. Two of the reasons: (1) Most syndicators like to establish working capital reserves (a darn good practice); and (2) investors are allowed to stage in capital contributions instead of paying one lump sum. In effect, investors are borrowing their equity contribution for a few years and will pay interest on this loan.

Acquisition fees should reflect the true nature of the property-buying process. Look at two examples: One syndicator acquires built, tenanted properties as high bidder through a real estate broker; another contacts a property owner, negotiates to buy from him directly and perhaps identifies an uncommon opportunity. The second syndicator provides added value and may be entitled to larger fees.

Also, the more functions the general partner performs, the more compensation he's entitled to. Some syndicators take no risk, acting as a "middle man" between a real estate broker and a securities dealer who finds investors. Others actually acquire the property as principal, renegotiate leases, change property managers, and refinance prior to syndication.

The timing of when the syndicator earns a profit from fees is important. If a profit is based only on the transaction occuring, or is paid in the early years, that can be worrisome. Investors probably haven't gotten all that they bargained for at that point, but the syndicator is making a profit. On the other hand, if the syndicator is receiving compensation early but only as reimbursement for costs and services, no harm is done.

You should look at "front-end fees" (fees paid during the pay-in period) as a percent of the total value of the real estate, not the equity capital contributions. The degree of mortgage leverage will distort the calculation if you don't. If fees are compensation for actual costs, front-end fees should decline relative to total real estate value as property size increases. The expense, cost and time involved in putting a transaction together are fairly similar regardless of the size of the transaction.

You should prefer "back-end" compensation—fees to the syndicator when the property is sold. This way the syndicator keeps his eye on the ball. The syndicator's incentive is parallel to the investor's economic interest. Back-end fees should be paid only after investors have received a reasonable return on cash investment.

In analyzing compensation, all fees to the syndicator at the back end of a transaction should be quantified in dollars and lumped together regardless of their label. On the basis of a hypothetical sale, you should determine the split of the total dollars between the limited partner and the syndicator. For a transaction with appreciation potential, the back-end split calculated this way should be in the range of 75%/25% or

80%/20% in the investor's favor. Transactions with limited appreciation potential should be closer to 90%/10%.

As we showed in Chapter 17, "markups" come in two forms. In one, the syndicator acquires the property and transfers it to the partnership at a higher price. Any cash resulting from a markup of this type should be added to the calculation of front-end fees. In another form, the markup is represented by debt, which is paid off from sale and refinancing proceeds. Here, the extra amount of the loan to be paid off should be added to back-end fees.

Comparing fees for different types of transactions may lead to erroneous conclusions. In transactions such as net leases and subsidized housing where significant residual value is not anticipated, most of the syndicator's fees will be at the front end. The only source of payment is capital contributions. Back-end fees should be low. On the other hand, where residual values can be significant, you should prefer lower front-end fees and be willing to pay higher back-end fees based on performance.

Fees should also vary based on the type of syndicator you're dealing with. A professional, ongoing syndication company may review hundreds of transactions for each one selected. Overhead costs are significant. Personnel often include mortgage financing experts, in-house legal and accounting staff, engineering talent, market and financial analysis experts, etc. You'll benefit from the "value added," but you also have to pay the cost.

Some partnership investments are put together by "hobby" syndicators, often lawyers or accountants whose main business is not syndication. Fees should be lower because the syndicator is not absorbing the cost of substantial ongoing overhead nor committing to provide investors the same kind of service.

Be sure you look at management fees paid to the syndicator. Investors could be overpaying. Apartment projects require significant hands on management. Properties subject to net lease are almost entirely run by the tenant. Larger properties generally don't entail a linear expansion in the cost of management.

Direct management should cost more than supervisory management.

Often in private placements, an asset management fee is charged. The function of asset management is extremely important. Be sure the service is performed. Asset management is preparing budgets, monitoring results, deciding about lease terms, refinancing and selling property, considering the financial condition of the partnership and distributing cash flow.

USE COMMON SENSE

A private placement is like a private party. Investors are invited to come in, but they have to pay a "cover charge" (fees). How big a cover charge investors are willing to pay depends mainly on how badly they want to get in. The best deals, combining sound economics and experienced sponsors, can command the highest fees.

You want to avoid dull parties with high cover charges. Use common sense. Basic business instinct and judgment are always the best predictors of success. Talk to other people who have been to previous parties thrown by the same people. Would they do it again?

CHAPTER 19

CHOOSE YOUR BENEFIT: SYNDICATION TRILOGY

This chapter is a parody on real estate syndication which shows how real estate transactions are "structured" for the particular markets in which they are syndicated. "Economic" and "tax" transactions are compared.

Got D. Dough, well-known real estate developer, is offering for sale his famous Pidgeon Run apartment complex in Pluckham, South Carolina. Dough made his reputation knowing how best to sell property. So, he contacted three syndicator friends: Phil Mypockets, Fat N. Happy and I. M. Greedy. Dough sent them a brochure on Pidgeon Run with the demographics of the area, conditions of the local economy, a listing of tenants and lease terms, pictures of the property and a pro forma financial projection of rents, expenses and cash flow (see Table I on the next page).

Pidgeon Run has operated successfully since opening five years ago and has produced a steadily increasing rental income. Operating expenses are under control and cash flow steadily increases. The project is worth $10,000 according to Dough. The mortgage loan, while at the attractive rate of 11%, is only in the amount of $6,000. Dough realizes the buyer will have to come up with a large amount of cash, $4,000, relative to property value, so he offers the property at an attractive free-and-clear capitalization rate of 10% (net operating income divided by the offering price).

TABLE I
PIDGEON RUN

	Year									
	1	2	3	4	5	6	7	8	9	10
Rents	$1,700	$1,836	$1,983	$2,142	$2,313	$2,498	$2,698	$2,914	$3,147	$3,398
Less: Operating Expenses	−700	−756	−816	−882	−952	−1,029	−1,111	−1,200	−1,296	−1,398
Net Operating Income	$1,000	$1,080	$1,167	$1,260	$1,361	$1,469	$1,587	$1,714	$1,851	$2,000
Less: Debt Service (Int. & Prin.)	−720	−720	−720	−720	−720	−720	−720	−720	−720	−720
Net Cash Flow	$ 280	$ 360	$ 447	$ 540	$ 641	$ 749	$ 867	$ 994	$1,131	$1,280
Adjustment For Non-Cash Items										
Subtract: Depreciation	−600	−600	−600	−600	−600	−600	−600	−600	−600	−600
Add: Principal Amortization	+60	+66	+73	+81	+89	+98	+108	+119	+131	+144
Taxable Income (Loss)	($ 260)	($ 174)	($ 80)	$ 21	$ 130	$ 247	$ 375	$ 513	$ 662	$ 824

NOTES: Purchase price of $10,000 was allocated 10% to land and 90% to buildings. Cash investment $4,000. The $6,000 balance was provided by an 11%, 25-year fully amortizing mortgage with a 12% debt service constant. Rents and expenses increase 8% per annum. Operating expense ratio starts at 41%. Depreciation was calculated on the straight-line method. Sale price was ten times Net Operating Income in the tenth year less remaining debt balance (original debt less principal amortization, sometimes called equity build-up).

PUBLIC OFFERING

Forty-eight hours after receiving the Pidgeon Run brochure, Phil Mypockets is in Dough's office. He has looked around the property with his engineering consultant, talked to a local appraiser about comparable property values and agrees on the spot to buy Pidgeon Run from Dough at the offering price.

Obviously, Mypockets is a syndicator of public offerings. Who else could come up with all that cash so fast? A nationwide brokerage firm, Y. R. House, sells Mypockets Property Fund like ice cream at a July 4th picnic. Last time out of the box the fund raised $45 million in 11.7 seconds.

To see if Dough's property would fit the requirements of the public fund, Mypockets adjusted Dough's pro forma to "gross up" the property for the fees and costs of the public offering. He also changed the method of depreciation (breaking out personal property from the building) and figured on deducting certain fees. Even at the adjusted cash price for the property of $5,542, Pidgeon Run shows a total return (cash flow plus tax savings) of more than 10% in the first year, building nicely to 13% to 14% in five years. Sale of the property ten years out, assuming modest growth, should provide the investor with a 14% internal rate of return. (See Table II on the next page.)

Mypockets showed the adjusted pro forma on the property to his firm's real estate department head, who gave the approval. Mypockets went to South Carolina to negotiate the purchase, and Dough listened patiently promising to get back to Mypockets in a week.

PRIVATE PLACEMENT

Next, Fat N. Happy calls Dough bearing glad tidings. Happy's overjoyed with the property and wants to put together a deal. Naturally, if Dough can figure out a way to stretch out payment of the large cash contribution over a period of years, Happy will pay handsomely. Happy realizes that if the property is producing more cash flow three or four years out when the purchase is completed, Dough is entitled to a purchase price higher than

TABLE II
PUBIC OFFERING

	Year									
	1	2	3	4	5	6	7	8	9	10
Pidgeon Run Net Operating Income (from Table I)*	$1,000	$1,080	$1,167	$1,260	$1,361	$1,469	$1,587	$1,714	$1,851	$2,000
Less: Debt Service	−720	−720	−720	−720	−720	−720	−720	−720	−720	−720
Property Cash Flow	$ 280	$ 360	$ 447	$ 540	$ 641	$ 749	$ 867	$ 994	$1,131	$1,280
Adjustment for Non-Cash Items										
Subtract: Depreciation	−800	−800	−800	−800	−800	−500	−500	−500	−500	−500
Amortized Fees	−164	−164	−164	−165	−165	—	—	—	—	—
Add: Principal Amortization	+60	+66	+73	+81	+89	+98	+108	+119	+131	+144
Taxable Income (Loss)*	($ 624)	($ 538)	($ 444)	($ 344)	($ 235)	$ 347	$ 475	$ 613	$ 762	$ 924

* Before allocations to General Partner.

NOTE: Equity contribution was recalculated for front-end load as follows: An acquisition fee equal to 6% of $10,000 original purchase price was added to $4,000 of cash investment. $4,600 was divided by .83 (5% working capital, 4% offering and organization costs and an 8% sales commission) to determine offering amount of $5,542. GP receives 10% of cash flow, 1% of taxable income or loss. From the Base Model, depreciation was increased in early years by allocating 10% of purchase price to land, 75% to building and 15% to personal property. Real and personal property depreciation was calculated on a straight-line method. An amount equal to acquisition fees and offering and organization costs was amortized over five years on the theory the GP could convert some hard costs to deductible items.

the current offering price. Happy realizes Dough will want to keep his hand in the management of the property during the pay-in period because he surely can't be expected to turn the property over to Happy until the whole purchase price has been paid.

Based on Dough's original projections, the property would produce $1,200 to $1,300 of net operating income three or four years out and would then be worth $12,000 to $13,000. Happy knows he will have to raise the ante for the property, but he hopes Dough will take back a note for some of the increase. Happy specializes in offering investors "risk-free transactions." So, he wants to give Dough all the cash flow from the property for three or four years in return for an ironclad guarantee against negative cash flow.

Before calling Dough, Happy contacted Jack Yorchain of S. O. Fistycated, Inc. to confirm the regional brokerage firm's appetite for a real estate private placement with "good economics." Yorchain liked the sound of Pidgeon Run and suggested that if the deal could be structured so that tax losses about equaled the limited partner capital contribution, then raising the equity in a private placement would be assured.

Based on paying a higher price for the property, depreciation deductions would increase. Happy decides to use accelerated depreciation to increase the tax loss in early years—a handy way to get Yorchain off his back about the level of tax deductions. Happy's trademark is being gentle to investors on the front end, where he takes no more than a standard real estate commission as an acquisition fee. To prove he's in the business for the long term, he says, most of his compensation will come from his 50% share of the appreciation after investors receive their money back in cash from sale or refinancing proceeds.

The transaction now fits all Happy's and Yorchain's requirements. Losses during the pay-in period almost equal the cash investment of $6,370. The cash-on-cash return in the second year after pay-in is completed is 8.9%. The slight increase in the mortgage from $6,000 to $7,500 ($1,500 taken back by

TABLE III
PRIVATE PLACEMENT

	Year									
	1	2	3	4	5	6	7	8	9	10
Pidgeon Run Net Operating Income (from Table I)	$1,000	$1,080	$1,167	$1,260	$1,361	$1,469	$1,587	$1,714	$1,851	$2,000
Less: Debt Service	-900	-900	-900	-900	-900	-900	-900	-900	-900	-900
Property Cash Flow	$ 100	$ 180	$ 267	$ 360	$ 461	$ 569	$ 687	$ 814	$ 951	$1,100
Cost of "No Negative Cash Flow" Guarantee From Seller	-100	-180	-267	-360	—	—	—	—	—	—
Cash Flow Before Other Non-Cash Items*	$ 0	$ 0	$ 0	$ 0	$ 461*	$ 569	$ 687	$ 814	$ 951	$1,100
Management Fee to Seller (1)	-115	-115	-115	-116	—	—	—	—	—	—
Depreciation	-1,484	-1,298	-1,206	-1,113	-1,020	-556	-556	-556	-556	-464
Amortized Fees	-199	-199	-199	-200	-200	—	—	—	—	—
Taxable Income (Loss)*	($1,798)	($1,612)	($1,520)	($1,429)	($ 759)	$ 13	$ 131	$ 258	$ 395	$ 636

* Before allocations to General Partner. Fifth-year cash flow is paid to seller for accrued Management Fee and not available for distribution.

(1) Accrued and paid in fifth year.

NOTE: Original transaction was assumed renegotiated to allow pay-in of equity contribution over four years. In the fourth year the net operating income is projected at $1,260 indicating a property value of $12,600 vs. $10,000 based on the first year. The GP agreed to pay $4,864 in cash ($4,000 purchase price plus $864 interest on deferred payments) and give a note to seller for $1,500 in the form of a 12% interest only wraparound for $7,500 (includes first mortgage of $6,000). Interest on deferred capital contributions was calculated at 13.3% interest. The purchase price of $12,364 ($7,500 mortgage loan plus $4,864 in cash) was increased by a 6% acquisition fee which increased the required equity contribution. The equity contribution required to purchase the property was divided by .88 to calculate the total equity contribution. No provision was made for working capital (compared to Public Offering Model) because of the seller's No Negative Cash Flow Guarantee. The seller manages the property during pay-in for an annual fee (accrued if not earned). In addition, the seller guarantees the partnership against operating losses for the first four years in return for the first four year's cash flow. Depreciation was recalculated on the higher purchase price (with the same percentage allocation to land, buildings and personal property as the Public Offering Model) on an accelerated method. The GP fees and syndication costs are calculated by the same method as the Public Offering Model including the assumed five year deductible items. The only exception is that in this structure the GP will receive 1% of cash flow.

Dough) will not hurt the economics much if the property appreciates. The tax lines do not cross (where tax on income exceeds cash flow) for more than twelve years. And, at 8% appreciation, Happy stands to put about half of the limited partner's capital contribution into his own pocket over the life of the deal. (See Table III on the previous page.)

"Are you sure this deal is saleable?" questions Dough. "I thought the magic number was 2-to-1, so the investor never had a dime at risk?" "Not out my way," replies Happy. "In the heartland, we go for sound economics and appreciation." Dough replies, "I'll let you know next week, Hap. Thanks for your fast answer. I like your proposal."

TAX LOSS STRUCTURE

The last to respond, I. M. Greedy, has a more difficult task than his competitors, for his objective is to produce the magic $2 of tax loss for every dollar of investment. For Greedy, no complication is too much to endure to achieve the nirvana of "no net investment." True heroics are required of the syndicator himself to produce the targeted tax result. Greedy's syndication distribution system is a group of financial planners, Could B. Gullible, Know X. Posure, Sy Yonara, Mark Updalot and Hugh G. Profit. With this bunch, tax loss is the most important selling tool. (Most of their sales take place between Thanksgiving and New Year's, and they usually spend January in the Caribbean.)

Greedy's starting point for his pro forma is the same deal Happy made with Dough. On top of that, Greedy must increase the leverage and stretch out the limited partner capital contribution to five years or more to yield the hoped-for tax result. (See Table IV on the next page.) The stretched-out capital contributions are financed by a second mortgage lender (secured also by investor notes). Greedy takes most of his compensation in the form of a mortgage on the property. The added leverage will increase the basis for depreciation. Both new notes accrue interest (increasing current deductions) and are paid off from

TABLE IV
TAX LOSS STRUCTURE

	Year									
	1	2	3	4	5	6	7	8	9	10
Cash Flow Before Other Non-Cash Items* (from Table III)	$ —	$ —	$ —	$ —	$ 461*	$ 569	$ 687	$ 814	$ 951	$1,100
Management Fees to Seller	-115	-115	-115	-116	—	—	—	—	—	—
Depreciation	-1,643	-1,429	-1,327	-1,225	-1,123	-612	-612	-612	-612	-510
Amortized Fees	-199	-199	-199	-200	-200	—	—	—	—	—
Syndicator Asset Management Fee	-45	-45	-45	-45	-46	—	—	—	—	—
Additional Interest—Accrued (1)	-471	-535	-608	-691	-784	-727	-749	-743	-733	-703
Taxable Income (Loss)*	($2,473)	($2,323)	($2,294)	($2,277)	($1,692)	($ 770)	($ 674)	($ 541)	($ 394)	($ 113)

* Before allocation to GP. Cash flow in fifth year is applied to unpaid accrued seller management fee. Cash flow of years 6 through 10 is applied to unpaid accrued interest obligations and is not available for distribution to LP's.

(1) Increment compared to Private Placement Model (Table III).

Note: Two additional financings were arranged which increased the total purchase price and hence depreciation and interest cost. A second mortgage from a savings and loan was arranged on a 13% interest only basis (accrues and adds to the balance owed if unpaid) for $1,500. $1,274 was used to allow the investor to stretch pay-in to five years, with the balance paid to the GP over five years as a Syndicator Asset Management Fee. The second mortgage is secured by investor notes representing pay-in obligations. The GP reduced his cash acquisition fee from 6% to 3% of the purchase price for a two-times larger fee (equity in his wraparound mortgage) which he will benefit from when the property is sold. The arrangement resulted in a new interest only wrap-around mortgage note of $8,400 (including the $7,500 seller wrap-around) accruing at 14% per annum (unpaid interest added to the balance). Other offering and organization costs and commissions calculated as for the Private Placement Model (Table III) except the GP is entitled to 25% of sale proceeds after return of cash investment in liquidation.

sale and refinancing proceeds rather than investor cash contributions or from the property's cash flow. (Greedy hasn't read the Tax ReformAct of 1984 yet. He'll be surprised when the IRS slaps him for income taxes due on the accrued interest.)

Here, the limited partner capital contribution of $6,503 is due over five years. Each dollar of pay-in is just about matched yearly with two dollars of tax loss. In order to service the additional leverage, all cash flow goes to the lenders, and the debt balance builds (because of the accrued interest feature) to about twice the original first mortgage. The investor still has a shot at a capital gain but only if appreciation is especially rapid. On the other hand, after tax, he has no money in the deal.

Dough says, "Greedy, you've done it again. Beautiful. Your syndication will sell out in a minute and a half." "I knew you'd like it," Greedy replies. "It's a deal only a fellow professional would understand." The two immediately agree to the transaction and order the lawyers to start work on the documents that afternoon.

BEHIND THE SCENES

To quote the old saw, "There's only so much juice in the orange." You have just been party to the process of syndicating a real estate property. Start with a pro forma on a property. Adjust for the impact of investor costs in a typical public offering. Take the deal private by deferring limited partner pay-in over a period of years. Carry the process of structuring for tax loss to its logical extreme. Through each step along the way, cash investment (or the price of the property) increases. The dollar amount of return decreases. Appreciation necessary to break even on sale heads north. The internal rate of return heads south. Syndicator benefits go up, and cash-on-cash return goes down.

Table V on the next page shows a comparison of economic benefits of each of the four ways of looking at this transaction. Notice changes in the level of cash flow, tax savings and net proceeds of sale for each one. Obviously, there is only so much

TABLE V
ECONOMIC BENEFITS NET TO INVESTOR
(After Tax)

Year	Pidgeon Run			Public Offering			Private Placement			Tax Loss Structure		
	Cash Flow	Tax (Cost) Savings	Total	Cash Flow	Tax (Cost) Savings	Total	Cash Flow	Tax (Cost) Savings	Total	Cash Flow	Tax (Cost) Savings	Total
1	$ 280	$ 130	$ 410	$ 252	$ 309	$ 561	$ —	$ 890	$ 890	—	$1,224	$1,224
2	360	87	447	324	266	590	—	798	798	—	1,150	1,150
3	447	40	487	402	220	622	—	752	752	—	1,136	1,136
4	540	(10)	530	486	170	656	—	708	708	—	1,127	1,127
5	641	(65)	576	577	116	693	—	376	376	—	838	838
6	749	(123)	.626	674	(172)	502	563	(6)	557	—	381	381
7	867	(188)	679	780	(235)	545	680	(65)	615	—	333	333
8	994	(256)	738	895	(303)	592	806	(128)	678	—	268	268
9	1,131	(331)	800	1,018	(378)	640	941	(195)	746	—	195	195
10	1,280	(412)	868	1,152	(457)	695	1,089	(315)	774	—	56	56
TOTALS	$7,289	($1,128)	$ 6,161	$6,560	($ 464)	$ 6,096	$4,079	$2,815	$ 6,894	—	$6,708	$6,708
Net Proceeds of Sale			+10,968			+10,353			+4,757			+2,790
Total Return			$17,129			$16,449			$11,651			$9,498
Original Cash Investment			$ 4,000			$ 5,542			$ 6,370			$6,503
Ratio of Return to Original Investment			4.3:1			3.0:1			1.8:1			1.5:1
Internal Rate of Return			19.0%			14.2%			11.5%			11.3%

Note: Table assumes investor is in the 50% tax bracket.

juice in the orange. You cannot maximize cash, tax and appreciation benefits simultaneously in a single real estate transaction.

In Dough's hands, Pidgeon Run shows almost $7,300 of cash flow over ten years and approximately $11,000 of sale proceeds based on an inflation rate of 8%. The cumulative tax is about $1,100 during the period. The total return is $17,000 compared to $4,000 of original cash investment. The internal rate of return is 19.0%.

My pocket's public offering alternative shows around $6,500 of cash flow and $10,000 of sale proceeds with a modest net tax cost during the ten-year period. The total return after tax is almost $16,500 compared to a $5,542 investment. The ratio of return to original investment is 3-to-1 and the internal rate of return is 14.2%.

Happy's economic private placement model shows about $4,000 of cash flow, $2,800 of tax savings and $4,800 of proceeds of sale after tax. The total return is $11,600 or 1.8 times the $6,370 cash investment. The internal rate of return is 11.5%

Greedy's tax loss structure shows no cash flow, $6,700 of tax savings and about $2,800 of sale proceeds after tax. The $9,500 total return is 1.5 times the $6,503 cash investment. The internal rate of return is 11.3%

Table VI on the next page shows fourteen different methods of comparing the four transactions. Notice the increasing amount of debt to which the property is subject and the increasing equity investment necessary to purchase the property. The public offering model shows the best investment economics, principally because the markups (in whatever form they take) are not as great as with the private placement alternatives. The difference between the transactions in total benefits measured in dollars is much greater than the difference between the rates of return. Conclusion: Pick the benefit you're aiming for and don't kid yourself. Corollary: Seeking tax benefits produces the best immediate result and the lowest overall rate of return.

TABLE VI
COMPARISON OF RESULTS

Item	Pidgeon Run	Public Offering	Private Placement	Tax Loss Structure
1. Equity	$ 4,000	$ 5,542	$ 6,370	$ 6,503
2. Debt Balance Ten Years Out	$ 5,031	$ 5,031	$ 7,500	$11,538
3. Purchase Price	$10,000	$11,542	$13,870	$16,403
4. Gross Rent Multiplier	5.9	6.8	8.2	9.6
5. Capitalization Rate on Net Operating Income	10%	8.7%	7.2%	6.1%
6. Cash-On-Cash Return	7%	4.6%	None	None
7. Years to Payback—Cash	7.2	9.1	Sale	Sale
8. Years to Payback—After Tax	7.3	9.2	9.3	8.2
9. Internal Rate of Return On Sale	19.0%	14.2%	11.5%	11.3%
10. Price to Cash Break Even	$ 9,031	$11,483	$13,871	$17,529
11. Break Even to Pidgeon Run Purchase Price	-9.7%	+14.8%	+38.7%	+75.3%
12. Net After-Tax Cash In Deal After Five Years	$ 1,550	$ 2,420	$ 2,846	$ 1,028
13. Total Investor Benefits (After Tax)	$17,129	$16,449	$11,651	$ 9,498
14. Total Syndicator Benefits (Pretax)	0	$ 3,261	$ 3,887	$ 4,952

NOTES: 1. Limited partner capital contribution.
2. Principal balance unpaid on mortgages at end of tenth year.
3. Equity plus debt on property at commencement date.
4. Purchase Price divided by gross rents.
5. First-year net operating income divided by Purchase Price.
6. First-year cash flow after debt service divided by Equity.
7. Point in years when cumulative cash distributions equal Equity.
8. Point in years when cumulative Economic Benefits after tax equal Equity.
9. The discount rate equating Equity in period zero (future pay-ins discounted to present value at 13.3%) with annual benefits after tax, and sale proceeds after tax in period 11.
10. Price on sale necessary to return 100% of Equity in Cash (pretax) after syndicator compensation.
11. #10 as a percent of Pidgeon Run Purchase Price ($10,000).
12. Equity, less 5-year cumulative economic benefits after tax.
13. & 14. Self-explanatory.

CHAPTER 20

FOUR WAYS TO MEASURE INVESTMENT VALUE

The two toughest problems partnership investors face are comparing a particular partnership investment's rate of return to other types of investments and comparing partnerships to each other. This is difficult for two major reasons. First, there are a number of ways of figuring a partnership's rate of return—some of which are misleading. (There's truth in the old adage that figures lie and liars figure!) Second, partnerships are complicated because they provide three kinds of returns: tax savings, cash distributions and capital gains. The rate of return calculations are difficult to make.

If you use rate-of-return methods to select and screen alternative partnership investments, you should follow these guidelines:

- **Compare investments using the same method.** Rates of return are often calculated differently. Using dissimilar rate-of-return methods on two investments makes direct comparisons impossible. For instance, some methods "net" investment pay-ins with benefits while others don't. The numbers will vary greatly.

- **Calculate rates of return on an after-tax basis.** The reason: Partnership benefits (tax savings, cash flow and gain on disposition of partnership assets) have varying tax consequences. Measuring benefits on an after-tax basis puts them on a common footing.

- **Compare returns for investments with similar risk levels.** New construction deals often show higher expected rates of return than commercial net leases. But, the projected net lease returns are more certain.

- **Compare returns for investments with similar economic benefits.** For example, if all the return is from tax savings, be sure that's the economic benefit needed, and compare the investment to other tax-saving investments. The return may be primarily from property appreciation. Be sure the investment objective is long term, and compare the investment with other net worth builders.

- **Set "hurdle" rates of return for each type of investment.** You'll save time. If an investment's return doesn't clear the hurdle, go no further.

- **Use the Adjusted Rate of Return ("ARR") to get the most realistic measure of value.** The ARR method allows you to compare accurately diverse types of investments based on individual financial situations.

Any quantitative approach to investment selection should be modified by qualitative considerations. Remember, rate-of-return measures are only as good as the underlying projections. Also, the business acumen of the general partner, terms of the offering and economic factors will ultimately determine partnership investment return. If tax savings are the important economic benefit, be sure proposed tax treatments are sound. If appreciation is the objective, you'll want have to be sure appreciation can be achieved.

Another qualitative consideration is matching investments with individual financial situations and goals. Tax-oriented deals generally assume tax savings are reinvested at high rates. Economic deals build net worth from appreciation within the partnership, but normally require investors to pay for some of the investment with after-tax capital.

In this chapter we'll show you strengths and weaknesses of four quantitative methods: internal rate of return, net investment internal rate of return, adjusted rate of return, and the present value of benefits-to-investment ratio. We'll also show you how to calculate each measure using the Hewlett-Packard HP-12C calculator.

INTERNAL RATE OF RETURN

The Internal Rate of Return ("IRR") is probably the most frequently used measure of investment value. The IRR is the rate which discounts after-tax economic benefits (tax savings, cash distributions and sale proceeds) to the present value of investment.

The IRR is not the compound annual growth rate of an investment. An investment with a 12% IRR will not necessarily double your money in 6 years like a 12% zero coupon bond. Said another way, you will double your money in six years in an investment with a 12% after-tax IRR only if you can reinvest annual benefits at a 12% after-tax rate. The higher the IRR, the greater the potential overstatement of the investment's benefits compared to your "real" return.

EXAMPLE 1
INTERNAL RATE OF RETURN

Year	"12% IRR Partners" Investment	Annual Economic Benefits	Bond Yielding 8.5% After Tax Investment	Annual Economic Benefits
1	$10,000	$ 0	$10,000	$ 0
2	—	5,000	—	850
3	—	3,000	—	850
4	—	1,800	—	850
5	—	1,500	—	850
6	—	900	—	850
7	—	500	—	850
8	—	330	—	10,850
Totals	$10,000	$13,030	$10,000	$15,950
REINVESTMENT EARNINGS*		$ 4,008		$ 1,184
NET WORTH IN YEAR 8*		$17,038		$17,134
AFTER-TAX INTERNAL RATE OF RETURN		12.0%		8.5%

*Assumes reinvested benefits earn 6% after tax per annum.

161

Here's an example: Which investment is better—a municipal bond yielding 8.5% after-tax or a partnership with a 12% after-tax IRR? Since the IRR in the municipal bond is 8.5%, the partnership looks better. But, the right answer depends on what you can earn reinvesting the annual benefits. If you reinvest the annual benefits at a 6% after-tax rate of return, the bond edges out the partnership in accumulating wealth. Your net worth builds to $17,134 with the bond versus $17,038 with the partnership investment on a $10,000 investment. (See Example 1 on the previous page.)

NET INVESTMENT INTERNAL RATE OF RETURN

The Net Investment Internal Rate of Return ("Net IRR") is similar to IRR except the annual investment pay-ins are reduced by annual economic benefits. The result: Net IRR is calculated on a much smaller investment amount producing a higher (sometimes meaningless) rate of return. (A 2-to-1 write-off deal can have an infinite Net IRR because the net investment could be zero.) When someone quotes you an extremely high rate of return on a real estate partnership investment, it's a good bet you are being shown the Net IRR. Watch out!

Suppose the investment in "12% IRR Partners" (left hand column of Example 1) is paid in four annual installments— $2,000, $5,000, $3,000 and $730. (See Example 2 on the next page.) The present value of the investment (discounted at 6%) is $10,000. By "netting" economic benefits in years two through four against the investment pay-ins, you reduce the "net" investment to $2,000. The result: The Net IRR jumps to 19.5%. Promoters love it.

ADJUSTED RATE OF RETURN

Using the Adjusted Rate of Return ("ARR"), you can compare partnership investments with each other and with alternative securities investments. And, you can get a more accurate feel for the "real" rate of return. Technically, the ARR is the

EXAMPLE 2
NET INVESTMENT INTERNAL RATE OF RETURN

	"12% IRR Partners" With Staged Investment Pay-Ins		
Year	Investment Pay-Ins	Annual Economic Benefits	Benefit/Cost Stream Used to Calculate Net IRR
1	$ 2,000	$ 0	$(2,000)
2	5,000	5,000	0
3	3,000	3,000	0
4	730	1,800	1,070
5	—	1,500	1,500
6	—	900	900
7	—	500	500
8	—	330	330
Totals	$10,730	$13,030	$ 2,300
NET INVESTMENT IRR			19.5%

rate that compounds the present value of all investment pay-ins to the sum of future benefits when benefits (tax savings plus after-tax cash flow) are reinvested at a "safe rate." Got that?

To make the ARR calculation, you pick the safe (reinvestment) rate to reflect actual after-tax returns available in the market. The IRR and Net IRR assume the after-tax reinvestment rate is the same as the overall rate of return on investment—12% and 19.5% in our examples. That's the fundamental weakness of IRR methods.

Returning to Example 1, the ARR is the compound rate equating the $10,000 investment (present value) with the total return, including reinvestment earnings. Using the ARR to evaluate the alternatives, you'd select the bond (with an ARR of 8.0%) over "12% IRR Partners" (with an ARR of 7.9%). That's the right choice since the bond investment provides greater net worth accumulation. (See Example 3 on the next page.)

PV BENEFITS/INVESTMENT RATIO

The Present Value of Benefits-to-Investment Ratio ("PV Benefits/Investment Ratio") is another valid way to rank investments. The ratio is simply the present value of benefits, dis-

EXAMPLE 3
ADJUSTED RATE OF RETURN

	"12% IRR Partners"			Bond Yielding 8.5% After Tax		
Year	Investment	Annual Economic Benefits	Earnings From Reinvestment of Benefits*	Investment	Annual Economic Benefits	Earnings From Reinvestment of Benefits*
1	$10,000	$ 0	$ 0	$10,000	$ 0	$ 0
2	—	5,000	—	—	850	—
3	—	3,000	300	—	850	51
4	—	1,800	498	—	850	105
5	—	1,500	636	—	850	162
6	—	900	764	—	850	223
7	—	500	864	—	850	287
8	—	330	946	—	10,850	356
Totals	$10,000	$13,030	$4,008	$10,000	$15,950	$1,184

TOTAL RETURN**	$17,038	$17,134
ADJUSTED RATE OF RETURN***	7.9%	8.0%

* Assumes reinvested benefits earn 6% after tax per annum.

** Total Annual Economic Benefits plus Total Earnings From Reinvestment.

*** Adjusted Rate of Return is the compound rate of return equating the present value of the investment to the sum of future benefits assuming benefits are reinvested at a "safe rate" of 6% after tax.

counted at a safe rate, divided by the present value of the investment amount. If the PV of Benefits/Investment Ratio exceeds 1-to-1, the projected return from the investment exceeds the "safe rate."

In our example, the present value of the investment amount in "12% IRR Partners" and in the bond is $10,000. The present value of benefits (discounted at the "safe rate" of 6%) is $11,395 for the bond and $11,330 for "12% IRR Partners." The PV Benefits/Investment Ratios are 1.139 and 1.133 respectively. (See Example 4 on the next page.)

You can combine the PV Benefits/Investment Ratio with a target rate of return to screen investments. Suppose you want to earn 12% after tax annually from your investments. Discount the benefits to present value at 12%, then compute the ratio. Investments with a ratio below 1-to-1 do not meet your required minimum return and should be rejected. (Continue to discount investment pay-ins to present value at the "safe rate.")

EXAMPLE 4
PV BENEFITS/INVESTMENT RATIO

	"12% IRR Partners"	Bond Yielding 8.5% After Tax
Present Value of Benefits*	$11,330	$11,395
Present Value of Investment*	$10,000	$10,000
PV BENEFITS/INVESTMENT RATIO	1.133	1.139

*Discounted at "safe rate" of 6% after tax.

The PV Benefits/Investment Ratio provides valid comparisons of alternative investments. But, ratios are hard to compare to market interest rates, so investors generally feel more comfortable with rate-of-return measures.

COMPARING RESULTS

These various measures produce strikingly different conclusions of investment value. (See the table below.) Rates of return range from 7.9% (the realistic ARR), to 12% (the IRR), to 19.5% (the aggressive Net IRR) for our sample partnership investment. The ARR or Present Value of Benefits-to-Investment Ratio are your best bets. You'll get fair comparisons and a realistic way to judge the return on any partnership investment versus securities investments.

RETURN COMPARISONS

	"12% IRR Partners"	Bond Yielding 8.5% After Tax
ARR	7.9%	8.0%
IRR	12.0%	8.5%
Net Investment IRR	19.5%	8.5%
Present Value of Benefits/Investment Ratio	1.133	1.139

MAKING THE CALCULATIONS

Now, let's see how to calculate all four measures step-by-step. (We'll assume you use a HP-12C calculator.) To help you make these calculations for offerings you evaluate, we've included a Stanger Rate-of-Return Calculation Worksheet at the end of this chapter.

The common approach to all calculations: Determine the periodic after-tax economic benefits from the financial projections; calculate the present value of the investment ("PVI")—the true cost of the investor's commitment; finally, figure a rate of return relating the PVI with the after-tax economic benefits.

Preliminary Steps—Begin by assembling the financial information on the particular investment you are considering. The typical private placement memorandum will contain financial projections, or you will have to estimate the partnership's economic benefits yourself. You'll need to know the amount and year of the economic benefits on an after-tax basis. We'll use the investment flow and benefits of Example 2 to show you the calculations. (See Table 1 below.)

As we indicated, calculating rates of return for partnership investments is complicated because they usually provide three kinds of benefit—tax savings, cash distributions and capital gains. You need to convert each projected benefit to an after-tax amount based on the investor's individual tax situation. If you expect the investor's situation to change significantly during the life of the investment, you may want to adjust the projections accordingly. For example, if you expect the investor's tax bracket to decline significantly in three or four years and you are considering a subsidized housing investment, be sure you reduce the projected tax savings (tax loss times expected tax bracket). Use the Worksheet at the end of this chapter to fine tune the after-tax benefits.

TABLE 1
HYPOTHETICAL PARTNERSHIP INVESTMENT

Year	Investment	After-Tax Economic Benefits
1	$ 2,000	$ 0
2	5,000	5,000
3	3,000	3,000
4	730	1,800
5	0	1,500
6	0	900
7	0	500
8	0	330
Totals	$10,730	$13,030

Once you have estimated the expected after-tax economic benefits, determine the present value of investment pay-ins, which is the true cost of the investment commitment. You want to track return on this amount. Use the so-called "safe rate" as the discount rate to calculate present value. A "safe rate" is the after-tax rate you could readily earn on an alternative investment, say short-term municipal bonds. The key is to choose a realistic rate and consistently use it for all investments you compare. In our examples, we use 6%.

Here are the HP-12C keystrokes to determine the present value of the investment based on the investment pay-ins shown in Table 1:

1. The initial investment is a current cash outlay, so this amount ($2,000 in year 1) is also the present value amount.

2. The next pay-in occurs one year later. Enter into the calculator the number $5,000; then press "CHS" (Change Sign); then press "FV" (Future Value).

3. Enter the number of periods this pay-in will be discounted (1 in this case); then press "N" (Number of Years).

4. Enter the "safe rate" discount, say 6%. Then press "i" (Percentage Interest Rate).

5. Press "PV" (Present Value) to get the present value of the second pay-in ($4,717).

6. Repeat these steps for each investment pay-in, and then add them up. The present value of the investment, or true cost, is $10,000.

Table 2 on the next page illustrates the results of the present value of investment calculation. You'll use the present value investment amount when calculating Internal Rate of Return, Adjusted Rate of Return and the Present Value of Benefits-to-Investment Ratio.

TABLE 2
CALCULATING PRESENT VALUE OF INVESTMENT

Year	(FV) Cash Pay-in	(N) Period Paid	(i) Discount Rate	(PV) Present Value
1	$ 2,000	0	6%	$ 2,000
2	5,000	1	6%	4,717
3	3,000	2	6%	2,670
4	730	3	6%	613
Totals	$10,730			$10,000

Internal Rate Of Return—The Internal Rate of Return ("IRR") is the rate which discounts after-tax economic benefits (shown in Table 1) to the present value of investment. Here are the keystrokes:

1. Enter the present value of the investment. Press $10,000, then press "CHS" and "g CFO."

2. Enter the first-year economic benefit (tax savings plus after-tax cash flow), $5,000 in our example, then press "g CFj." Repeat this step for each yearly benefit shown in Table 2.

3. Press "f," then "IRR." After several seconds of calculating, the machine will display the after-tax IRR which is 12.02%.

Net Investment Internal Rate Of Return—The Net Investment Internal Rate of Return ("Net IRR") is calculated similarly to IRR except the annual investment pay-ins are reduced by annual economic benefits. The rate of return is then calculated using this reduced investment amount and the "net" economic benefits.

Here's how the Net IRR is calculated. First, determine the annual "net" economic benefits by adding tax savings plus after-tax cash flow and subtracting investment. (See Table 3 on the next page.)

TABLE 3
CALCULATING NET IRR

Year	Investment	After-Tax Economic Benefit	Net After-Tax (Cost) Benefit
	(1)	(2)	(Column 2 Minus Column 1)
1	$2,000	$ 0	$(2,000)
2	5,000	5,000	0
3	3,000	3,000	0
4	730	1,800	1,070
5	0	1,500	1,500
6	0	900	900
7	0	500	500
8	0	330	330
Totals	$10,730	$13,030	$ 2,300

Then, use these keystrokes:

1. Enter the first-year Net Cost amount ($2,000), then press "CHS" and "g CFO."

2. Enter the second year's Net Benefit, then press "g CFj." When a Net Cost is projected (versus a Net Benefit), press "CHS" then "g CFj." In this example, press 0, then "g CFj." Repeat this step for each yearly Net Benefit (Cost).

3. Press "f," then "IRR." After several seconds of calculating, the machine will display the Net Investment IRR (19.48%).

Remember: Avoid this method. Reducing partnership investment by the benefits received makes no more sense than reducing a bond investment by the interest payments. The result is a gross overstatement of return. The Net IRR in our example is 19.48%—more than one and a half times the IRR. The reason: "net" investment over the first four years totals only $930 versus the $10,000 present value of the investment.

Adjusted Rate Of Return—The Adjusted Rate of Return ("ARR") is your best tool for accurately comparing partnership investments with each other and with alternative securities investments. When you calculate the ARR, you are finding the rate that compounds the present value of all investment pay-ins to the sum of future benefits when benefits are reinvested at a "safe rate."

First, compound the annual after-tax benefits (shown in Table 1) forward to their future value at the end of the investment period using the "safe rate." Here are the steps:

1. Enter $5,000, the Economic Benefit in year 2; then press "CHS" and "PV."

2. Enter 6%, the "safe rate," then press "i."

3. Enter 6, the reinvestment period then press "N." The reinvestment period is the number of years from receipt of the economic benefit until the sale of the investment.

4. Press the "FV" button. The calculator will display $7,093, the future value of the economic benefit in year 2 including the earnings from reinvesting the benefit until year 8.

5. Calculate the future value of each subsequent year's economic benefit by following steps 1 through 4; and then add them up. The total value of reinvested benefits is $17,038 in our example.

Table 4 shows the results of these calculations.

TABLE 4
CALCULATING THE FUTURE VALUE OF REINVESTED BENEFITS

Year	(PV) Economic Benefits (from Table 1)	(i) Reinvestment Rate	(N) Number of Reinvestment Periods	(FV) Future Value of Economic Benefits
1	$ 0	6%	7	$ 0
2	5,000	6%	6	7,093
3	3,000	6%	5	4,015
4	1,800	6%	4	2,272
5	1,500	6%	3	1,787
6	900	6%	2	1,011
7	500	6%	1	530
8	330	6%	0	330
Totals	$13,030			$17,038

The ARR is the compound rate that equates the present value of the investment pay-ins ($10,000) with the future value of reinvested benefits ($17,038). Here's how you calculate the ARR:

1. Enter the present value of the investment pay-ins ($10,000 in our example); press the "CHS" button; then press the "PV" button.

2. Enter 7 (the number of years the investment was held); then press the "N" button.

3. Enter $17,038 (the total future value of reinvested benefits); then press the "FV" button.

4. Press the "i" button. The ARR is 7.9%, the rate of return on your investment assuming reinvestment of benefits at 6%. In other words, if you invest $10,000 at a rate of 7.9% compounded annually, you will accumulate $17,038 in seven years.

Present Value Of Benefits-To-Investment Ratio—The Present Value of Benefits-to-Investment Ratio also provides valid comparisons of alternative investments. To derive the ratio, simply divide the present value of benefits (discounted at a "target" after-tax return rate) by the present value of the investment (discounted at the "safe" rate). If the ratio exceeds 1-to-1, then the investment's rate-of-return is greater than the "target" return.

Start by determining the present value of partnership benefits. Use the same keystrokes you used to calculate the present value of the investment. The results are shown in Table 5 on the next page assuming a "target" rate of return of 6% after tax.

Next, divide the present value of benefits by the present value of the investment, $10,000. The resulting ratio is 1.13:1 confirming that the investment's rate of return exceeds the target rate.

TABLE 5
CALCULATING PRESENT VALUE OF BENEFITS

Year	(FV) Benefit	(N) Period Received	(i) Discount Rate	(PV) Present Value
1	$ 0	0	6%	$ 0
2	5,000	1	6%	4,717
3	3,000	2	6%	2,670
4	1,800	3	6%	1,511
5	1,500	4	6%	1,188
6	900	5	6%	673
7	500	6	6%	352
8	330	7	6%	219
Totals	$13,030			$11,330

You can use the Stanger Rate-of-Return Calculation Worksheet on the following pages to calculate Adjusted Rate of Return and Internal Rate of Return, the two most commonly used measures.

STANGER RATE–OF–RETURN CALCULATION WORKSHEET

This worksheet shows you how to calculate an investment's rate of return. Blank forms are provided to enter the data you need. Our easy to follow step-by-step process sets forth keystroke instructions for use with Hewlett-Packard hand held calculators. We show both Adjusted Rate of Return and Internal Rate of Return calculations, so you'll be able to compare investments by both rate-of-return methods.

Present Value of Investment

Year	FV Cash Paid	N Period Date	i Safe Rate	PV Present Value Of Investment
	$	0	%	$
	$	1	%	$
	$	2	%	$
	$	3	%	$
	$	4	%	$
	$	5	%	$
	$	6	%	$
	$	7	%	$
	$	8	%	$
TOTAL	$			$

Determine the Present Value of Your Investment:

1. Your initial investment is a current cash outlay so the amount of the investment is also the present value amount. Enter this number in the first line under Cash Paid as well as under the "Present Value of Investment" column on the form above.

2. List on the form each subsequent investment pay-in in the period in which it occurs.

3. Enter into the calculator the amount of the second investment pay-in. Press the "CHS" (Change Sign) button; then press "FV" (Future Value) button.

4. Enter the number of the period in which this investment is paid; then press the "N" (Number of Periods) button.

5. Enter the discount rate (the safe rate); then press the "i" (Percentage Interest Rate) button.

6. Press the "PV" (Present Value) button which will give you the present value of the second pay-in. Enter the answer in the second line under the Present Value Column.

7. Repeat Steps 3 through 6 for each investment pay-in and then add them up. The total is the present value of the investment.

STANGER RATE-OF-RETURN CALCULATION WORKSHEET (continued)

Value of Economic Benefits

Year	Taxable Loss (Income)	×	Tax Rate	=	Tax Savings (Cost)	+	Cash Flow	+	After-Tax Proceeds From Sale of Assets	=	PV Total Economic Benefits	i Safe Rate	N Periods Until Sale	FV Adjusted Future Value of Economic Benefits
	$				$		$		$		$	%		$
	$				$		$		$		$	%		$
	$				$		$		$		$	%		$
	$				$		$		$		$	%		$
	$				$		$		$		$	%		$
	$				$		$		$		$	%		$
	$				$		$		$		$	%		$
	$				$		$		$		$	%		$
	$				$		$		$		$	%		$
	$				$		$		$		$	%		$
	$				$		$		$		$	%		$
	$				$		$		$		$	%		$
TOTAL	$				$		$		$		$	%		$

Determine the Economic Benefits of the Investment

1. List the investment's projected Taxable Loss (Income) for each year; then multiply by your assumed tax rate. The result is the amount of Tax Savings per year.

2. Add the investment's projected Tax Savings, Cash Flow and After-Tax Sales Proceeds for each year. The sum is the investment's Total Economic Benefits per year. Enter these amounts in the first several columns in the worksheet on the next page. For real estate investments the After-Tax Sales Proceeds are calculated as follows: Cash from Sale of Property plus Cumulative Tax Loss and Cumulative Cash Flow less Cash Investment equals Taxable Gain. Calculate Taxes Due on Sale. Subtract Taxes Due on Sale from Cash from Sale of Property to find After-Tax Sales Proceeds.

Calculate the Adjusted Future Value of Economic Benefits

1. Enter the amount of the first year's Economic Benefit; press "CHS" button; then press "PV" button.

2. Enter the safe rate, then press "i";

3. Enter the Reinvestment Period, then press "N." The Reinvestment Period is the number of years from receipt of the Economic Benefit until the sale of the investment. If you are estimating the sale of an investment seven years after the first pay-in of original investment, the Reinvestment Period will be six years for an Economic Benefit received in the second period. The second period can be the same year as the year of original investment.

4. Press the "FV" button and the calculator will then display the future value of the first economic benefit taking into account the earnings of reinvesting the benefit at the "safe" rate until the investment is sold. This is the Adjusted Future Value of Economic Benefits.

5. Calculate the future value of each year's Economic Benefit by following Steps 1 through 4, and then add them up.

Calculate the Adjusted Rate of Return

1. Enter the total Present Value of Investment from Step One; press the "CHS" button; then press the "PV" button.

2. Enter the number of years the investment was held; then press the "N" button.

3. Enter the total Adjusted Future Value of Economic Benefits; then press the "FV" button.

4. Press the "i" button. The machine will then calculate the Adjusted Rate of Return, the compound rate of return on your investment assuming reinvestment of benefits at the "safe" rate.

Calculate the Internal Rate of Return

1. Enter the total Present Value of Investment from Step One. Then press (in order) the buttons, CHS and g CFO.

2. Enter the first yearly Economic Benefit; then press the button g Cfj.

3. Repeat Step Two for each Economic Benefit in order from the first one received to the last.

4. Press f, then IRR. After several minutes of calculating, the machine will display the IRR.

CHAPTER 21

REAL ESTATE PRIVATE PLACEMENT EVALUATION CHECKLIST

Evaluating private placements becomes easier if you use a consistent methodology. You'll also develop your own critical screening factors more quickly by standardizing the measures you use to compare deals. The "Private Placement Evaluation Checklist" on the following pages is a uniform method to measure each deal you analyze. An added bonus: By having these forms for many deals, you have a handy reference file for quickly comparing investments.

Here are some tips for how you can get the Checklist filled out:

- Submit the Checklist through the department of your broker/dealer which coordinates direct participation investments.

- If you are an independent, form a "due diligence" group with other financial advisors. Develop a form letter stating the total fundraising potential of the group. You'll find that many other advisors have the same problems and interests you do in evaluating private placements.

- If you are requesting information for your own use and you are not acting as a registered representative (e.g., you are an accountant reviewing an offering), state that you must have this information to fulfill your roll as an "offeree representative," and the investment currently under active consideration can't be approved without the information.

NAME OF OFFERING _____

TOTAL OFFERING SIZE $ _____   UNIT SIZE $ _____

SPONSOR _____

ADDRESS _____

CONTACT _____ PHONE _____

ASSET

QUALITY

Property Name and Address _____

_____

Property Type   _____

Location

Grade (excellent, good, fair or poor)   _____

Physical Condition

Age   _____
Maintenance Condition (ie, good, etc.)   _____
Construction (wood, brick, steel)   _____
Style   _____
Marketability (size of units, # of
  bedrooms, etc. vs. market)   _____
Inspection Report and Engineering
  Study Performed?   _____ (Y,N)
Required Property Improvements _____

_____

_____

Economic Factors

Lease Terms:
  Duration (Anchor Tenants)   _____ (yrs.)
  Current Rental Rates (per unit, sq.ft.) $ _____
  Current Occupancy   _____ %
  Occupancy Necessary to Break Even   _____ %
  Going Rental Rate in Market $ _____
  Credit Quality of Tenants _____

_____

_____

Financing Terms:
   Loan Maturities   _____ (yrs.)
   Interest Rate(s)   _____ %
   Lender Participations (describe) _____

_____

_____

Market Trends:
   Comparable Available Sq. Ft.
     in Market   _____ sq. ft.
   New Space Under Construction   _____ sq. ft.
   Occupancy Rates for Similar Space   _____ %
   Absorbtion Rate Per Annum   _____ sq. ft.

VALUE

Prices of Comparable Property

Per Sq. Ft. (or Unit) $ _____ sq. ft.
Gross Rent Multipliers
   (Purchase Price ÷ Gross Rents)   _____
Capitalization Rates
   (Net Operating Income ÷ Purchase Price) _____ %

Price of Partnership Property

Price Paid by LPs Per Sq. Ft. (or Unit) $ _____
Gross Rent Multiplier   _____
Purifier Capitalization Rate   _____ %
   (Net Operating Income ÷ Purchase Price
    Paid by LPs)
Appraised Value $ _____
Projected Property IRR   _____ %

Seller Financing Terms _____

_____

_____

General Partner Guarantees _____

_____

_____

SPONSOR

QUALIFICATIONS

Personnel and Staffing (Top Management)

Number of Executive Personnel   _____

Average Years of Real Estate Experience   _____ yrs.

Average Length of Service with Syndicator _____ yrs.

Acquisition Staff

Number of Professional Personnel   _____

Average Years of Acquisition Experience   _____

Acquisition Procedures and Criteria

Describe: _____

_____

_____

Number of Acquisitions Per Year   _____

Pro Forma Financials Prepared?   _____ (Y,N)

Comparable Property Analysis
Performed?   _____ (Y,N)

Management and Legal Departments
Involved?   _____ (Y,N)

Acquire through: Developers?   _____ (Y,N)

                Brokers?   _____ (Y,N)

Involvement of Senior Personnel?   _____ (Y,N)

Involvement of Property Management
Personnel?   _____ (Y,N)

Property Management Staff

Average Years of Property
Management Experience   _____ yrs.

Third Party Management Agents used?   _____ (Y,N)

Describe Checks/Monitoring of Agents'
Performance (Budgets, Variances, etc.): _____

_____

_____

_____

Legal Staff

Number   _____

Averages Years of Experience   _____ (yrs)

LP Recordkeeping, IRS and SEC Reporting   _____

_____

_____

Experience of Senior CFO _____

_____

_____

PRIOR PERFORMANCE

Total Dollars Raised in Syndications $ _____

Number of Partnerships Formed   _____

Number of Partnerships Liquidated   _____

Internal Rate of Return to LPs in
    Partnerships Liquidated   _____ %

Number of Properties Bought (of like kind) _____

Number of Properties Sold (of like kind)   _____

Average Annual Gain (on property sales)   _____ %

FINANCIAL CONDITION

Net Worth of GP $ _____

Current Ratio   _____

Net Worth of Parent of GP $ _____

Bank References: _____

_____

_____

PROGRAM

TERMS

Front-End Fees (% of LP Capital)   _____ %

Contingency Reserves (% of LP Capital)
    At Program Inception   _____ %
    In Year Following Pay-in Period   _____ %

Reserves for Capital Improvements
    (% of LP Capital)   _____ %

Internal Rate of Return on Property   _____ %

Internal Rate of Return to LP   _____ %

Present Value of LP Benefits-to-
    Investment Ratio   _____

Property Cost (All Payments to Seller) $ _____

All LP Cash Contributions Plus
    Debt Assumed $ _____

Property "Markup"   _____ %

Appreciation Necessary to Break Even   _____ %

Stanger Offering Terms Rating   _____

Evaluating a Private Placement

FEASIBILITY

Reasonableness of Assumptions in Projections
Length of Rent-Up Period   _____ yrs.
Cash Flow to LP in First Year   _____ %
Annual Rate of Rental Increase   _____ %
Annual Rate of Expense Increase   _____ %
Capitalization Rate on Sale   _____ %
"Forecasting" Opinion Provided by
  CPA firms?   _____ (Y,N)

Accountants Opinion on Tax Issues_____
_____
_____

ECONOMIC VALUE

ARR (or IRR)   _____ %
Payback Period   _____ yrs

RISK

Relative Risk Factor (odds of success)   _____

RISK ADJUSTED EXPECTED RETURN

Economic Value (Rate of Return)
  X Risk Factor   _____

182

SECTION IV

EVALUATING THE SPONSOR

CHAPTER 22

ASKING THE RIGHT QUESTIONS

The purpose of the Sponsor Information Questionnaire presented in this chapter is to shed light on how the sponsor organization of a real estate partnership operates. Highlighted are the methods the sponsor uses to make real estate investments, the size and scope of operations compared to personnel, the solvency and liquidity of the sponsor, and the independent third parties with whom the sponsor generally deals. The Sponsor Information Questionnaire will help you solicit and organize the minimum information on sponsors necessary to make sound investment decisions. In addition, you'll get a good idea how squared away the sponsor is by the nature and timeliness of his response to the Questionnaire.

The prospectus only reveals the static condition of the sponsor—a snapshot of an organization at a point in time. And, the document often allows the sponsor wide latitude in the conduct of operations. The reason: so the sponsor can perform freely without undue restriction in the future.

The Questionnaire will help you elicit useful information on the dynamic condition of the organization and the actual operating policies followed—especially important in light of the rapidly increasing scale of operations of most limited partnership sponsors. Sponsors should have answers readily available because they are accustomed to addressing these important issues in presentations to investors and brokers. Also, the typical due diligence investigation will zero in on these areas and many others.

When you are considering several different programs, you can use the Questionnaire as your interview outline. Or, send it to the sponsor to fill out for you. Ask these questions to the wholesaler to see how much he really knows about the offering. In either case, when you ask the right questions, the people you are dealing with will respect you and will realize that they have to give you straight answers. Remember, as a potential investor or advisor, you're entitled to answers for all of the following areas of inquiry. Depending on the answers, you'll quickly begin to discern qualitative differences between the sponsors you are investigating.

The Sponsor Information Questionnaire is divided into five parts.

- **Management**—The Questionnaire describes the founders, senior officers and key individuals. Such areas as education, experience, employment history and compensation are covered. An organization chart will also show changes in personnel and key functions in the last two years. You'll have an idea of longevity and stability of the executive corp. The conflicts of interest policy will be described.

- **Organization and Procedures**—Information on the sponsor organization, subsidiaries, affiliates, and cross ownership is presented. The history of the business and its current size are described. Operating policies concerning origination of property acquisitions, property management, investment decision-making and investment criteria are outlined. A set of investor communications and reports is requested so you can judge the adequacy of limited partner reporting. The staff for marketing to broker/dealers is described.

- **Financial Condition**—Solvency, liquidity, sponsor net worth and material adverse events are uncovered here. "Solvency" refers to the change in the balance sheet over several years and any contingent liabilities or other contractual obligations and guarantees. Working capital, lines of credit, borrowing capacity, debt maturities and cash flow projections make up the "Liquidity" portion. In the event the partnership has a sole corporate general partner, the calculation of "Net Worth" to meet the IRS "safe harbour" test is requested. The "Material Adverse Events" portion deals with litigation, bankruptcies, foreclosures and defaults at both the sponsor and partnership level.

- **Performance Record**—This section shows types of offerings and properties purchased in the past, the size and number of partnerships, and the amount of properties purchased. Acquisition activities anticipated for the current or succeeding year are compared with past levels. Information is requested on the success and efficiency of fundraising and procedures followed for private placements.

- **Industry Standing and Reputation**—Outside parties with whom the sponsor deals are enumerated. The list includes attorneys, accountants, independent directors, stockbrokers, lenders, co-developers, joint venture partners, major tenants, appraisers and other outside consultants. A description of litigation and disputes with the IRS is requested.

The Questionnaire helps you determine how the sponsor's organization actually functions. Due to the rapidly increasing scale of operations of most limited partnership sponsors, one of the key questions about the industry is whether the pace of expansion has been too much for internal personnel and procedures to handle properly. The Questionnaire shows you how the sponsor organizes and plans his business as well as how he has handled change in the past several years.

SPONSOR INFORMATION QUESTIONNAIRE

Unless the text indicates otherwise, the questions are about the parent sponsor organization, not the subsidiary general partner or the limited partnership.

I. Management
A. Indicate principals, senior officers and key acquisition and property management department personnel. List the following information for each individual:
1. Name, title, age, education and credentials, percentage or nature of ownership.
2. Years with the company, years in present position, personal relationships with others in management.
3. Previous employment history, past or present positions (directorships, associations, government bodies).
B. Describe nature and basis of incentive compensation and employment agreements.
C. Provide organization chart, indicating changes of personnel or key functions in last two years.
D. Describe conflicts of interest policy relative to limited partnerships.

II. Organization and Procedures
A. State the legal form of the firm (corporation, partnership), and include a chart showing parent companies, subsidiaries, and divisions, with ownership noted. Indicate ownership by outsiders.
B. State the location of headquarters and list other offices, indicating primary purpose of each (acquisition, marketing, etc.).
C. Indicate the current number of employees in total and in each functional capacity. Compare with one year and three years ago.
D. Give a description and history of the business, and state what distinguishes the company from its competitors.
E. Describe operating policies. How do you originate acquisitions and what are your investment criteria? Describe the investment decision-making process. How

do you manage properties and resolve conflicts of interest between competing programs?

F. List major program, organizational and acquisition policy changes in the last three years.

G. Provide the latest management letter from your independent accountant.

H. Provide a set of investor communications and reports for a previous partnership and describe how you deal with limited partner complaints and requests.

I. Describe your marketing staff and the type and level of assistance provided to a broker/dealer.

III. Financial Condition
A. Solvency:
1. Balance sheet for last three years.
2. Contingent liabilities, unfunded contractual obligations; indicate security or guarantees for loans.
B. Liquidity:
1. Working capital.
2. Credit lines, borrowing capacity and name of major bank.
3. Near-term debt maturities.
4. Cash flow projection for next 12 months.
C. Show the calculation of the net worth requirement and adequacy of net worth for "safe harbour" purposes if there is a sole corporate general partner.
D. Material Adverse Events:
1. Litigation, convictions, recision offers.
2. Bankruptcies, foreclosures, defaults, forced liquidations.
3. Discuss events, causes and results of accommodations with creditors at the limited partnership level.

IV. Performance Record
A. Areas of expertise: Kinds of offerings, typical objectives, types of property, locations.
B. Volume in total for the current year and per year for at least the last five years:
1. Number of partnerships and amounts raised in total, and in public and private offerings.

2. Number of participating investors.

3. Number and gross price of properties and units purchased.

C. Plans and Events: Number and gross price of properties to be purchased, and total equity to be raised and invested in the current or succeeding year.

D. Efficiency:

1. Average months between offering date and closing date.

2. Amounts raised as percent of amounts offered.

3. Average months between closing date and full investment of proceeds.

4. Average months between closing date and beginning of cash distributions from operations.

5. Number of months, if any, in the last two years that you had two or more programs with similar objectives and criteria competing with each other for acquisitions.

E. Private Placements: Discuss your procedures for marketing private placements and furnish opinion of counsel that private placements in past year did not require registration.

F. Indicate percentage of repeat customers (investors participating in more than one offering).

V. Industry Standing and Reputation

A. List attorneys and accountants names and affiliations of independent directors and state changes and reason for changes in the past five years.

B. List major broker/dealers and changes in the past three years.

C. List major institutional lenders, co-developers, major property sources, joint venture partners, major credit tenants.

D. List major appraisers or other outside consultants.

E. Describe significant disputes with the IRS and their resolution.

GETTING THE ANSWERS

Yes, the Questionnaire is lengthy—deliberately so. Even if you don't succeed in getting answers to all the questions, you may find out something more important: the sponsor's attitude toward public disclosure. Regrettably, some sponsors don't like to reveal anything unless SEC-required. You don't need to know anything else about these organizations—avoid them. On the other hand, a surprising number of successful sponsors will take the time to answer legitimate requests for information.

To obtain results, send the Questionnaire to the sponsor along with a personalized cover letter indicating your desire to become better acquainted. It's a good idea to indicate that you will welcome wholesalers or marketing representatives but only **after** you have received written answers to the questions enclosed.

CHAPTER 23

ANALYZING AND COMPARING SPONSOR TRACK RECORDS

The real estate limited partnership industry supplies a wealth of information on property and partnership performance. However, the method of presentation accepted by the SEC for public programs seems largely unintelligible both to pros and neophytes. The lack of standardization of reporting to investors compounds the difficulty of making valid comparisons. Conventional wisdom says you should invest with a sponsor who has a good track record. Making that determination is at best a monumental job and at worst impossible.

This chapter presents a method for making the best of prospectus data and supplies forms and worksheets for standardized, in-depth evaluation of a sponsor's "track record."

HOW TO READ PRIOR PERFORMANCE TABLES

Despite their limitations, "Prior Performance Tables" found in the prospectus of a public program can provide some useful information to help you judge results of liquidated partnerships and the sponsor's ability to manage properties effectively and realize gains on property sales. Here are the five types of tables and what you can learn from them. (Offering Memoranda of private programs may provide tables similar to those found in a public program prospectus.)

Table I—Documents the sponsor's "Experience In Raising And Investing Funds." Skip it entirely.

Table II—Outlines "Compensation To Affiliates" of the general partner. Skip it entirely.

Table III—Outlines the "Operating Results Of Prior Partnerships." (See example below.) Here comes the important part. You should look at the trend of "Cash Generated From Operations." You want to see increasing cash flow which is the result of increasing rents and net operating income. The reason: Property is worth a multiple of operating cash flow. Rising cash

TABLE III

OPERATING RESULTS OF PRIOR PUBLIC PARTNERSHIPS

(Dollars in 000's except for amounts per $1,000 investment)

	Public Partners IV		
	1985	1984	1983
Gross revenues	$3,182	$2,817	$2,468
Profit on sale of properties	None	None	None
Less:			
Operating expenses	770	760	754
Interest expense	0	0	0
Depreciation	245	259	326
Net income (loss)—GAAP basis	$2,167	$1,798	$1,388
Taxable income (loss) from operations	$1,999	$1,648	$1,322
Cash generated from operations	**$2,244**	**$1,907**	**$1,648**
Cash generated from sales	0	0	0
Cash generated from refinancing	0	0	0
Cash generated from operations, sales and refinancing	$2,244	$1,907	$1,648
Less: Cash distributions to partners	**1,919**	**1,641**	**1,465**
Cash generated after cash distributions	$ 325	$ 266	$ 183
Federal income tax results per $1,000 investment:			
Ordinary income (loss)—operations	$ 198	$ 163	$ 131
Capital gain	0	0	0
Cash distributions per $1,000 investment:			
Source (GAAP basis) Investment income	$ 190	$ 163	$ 138
Return of capital	0	0	7
Total	$ 190	$ 163	$ 145
Source (cash basis) Sales and refinancing	$ 0	$ 0	$ 0
Operations	190	163	145
Total	$ 190	$ 163	$ 145
Amount remaining invested in partnership properties at end of 1985	100.0%		

flow means rising property values. Next, look at "Cash Distributions To Partners" versus "Cash Generated From Operations." If distributions exceed cash generated, reserves are being reduced to provide current cash return—a risky practice. The distributions must be coming from operations, not reserves, to be meaningful. Look at "Cash Distributions Per Thousand Dollars Of Investment" and the trend of distributions.

Table IV—Shows "Results of Completed Public Partnerships" (prior partnerships completely liquidated), a good indication of results you may expect. Here, you'll see the time involved from commencement of activities until liquidation. You can calculate the approximate level of total after-tax return enjoyed by past limited partners. You add all the economic benefits after tax (tax savings, cash flow, gain on sale) and subtract taxes due on sale.

Begin by calculating tax consequences of the investment from information under "Federal Income Tax Results." (See Table IV on the next page.) Start with Tax Savings during the operating phase, which equal one-half the "Ordinary Loss From Operations" (line #1a) for a 50% tax bracket investor. Then, multiply "Capital Gain" (line #2) and "Deferred Capital Gain" (line #3a) by the capital gain tax rate (say 20%) and subtract the result from Tax Savings. Then subtract one-half the "Ordinary Income From Recapture" (line #1b). Finally, add in the total cash distributions received by limited partners (line #6c) and the Equity in Notes Received At Sale (line #7).

The resulting amount, $3,016, is the limited partner's total after-tax return per $1,000 invested. The length of time from formation of the partnership to sale of the last property was seven years and three months. You tripled your investment in that period of time. Quite a successful investment. Remember, your return over your original investment is $2,016 and $590 of that return is in notes.

Table V—Using the "Sales of Properties in Prior Public Programs" table, you can figure the appreciation on total property cost and the appreciation on equity investment. Compare

TABLE IV
RESULTS OF COMPLETED PUBLIC PARTNERSHIPS
(Dollars in 000's except for amounts per $1,000 investment)

	Public Partners II
Dollar amount raised:	$12,505
Number of properties purchased:	8
Date of closing of offering:	12–20–75
Date of first sale of property:	10–14–79
Date of final sale of property:	3–05–82
Federal income tax results per $1,000 investment:	
(1) Ordinary income (loss):	
(a) From operations	$(1,640)
(b) From recapture	500
(2) Capital gain:	$1,800
(3) Deferred gain:	
(a) Capital	$1,670
(b) Ordinary	0
Cash distributions per $1,000 investment:	
(5) Source (GAAP basis):	
(a) Investment income	$2,550
(b) Return of capital	0
(c) Total	$2,550
(6) Source (cash basis):	
(a) Sales and refinancing	$1,950
(b) Operations	600
(c) Total	$2,550
(7) Equity in Notes Received At Sale:	$ 590

"Total Selling Price" (column #5 in Table V on the next page) with "Total Cost" (column #8) for all properties to judge the average appreciation on total property investment. To determine the average appreciation on the equity investment, subtract "Total Cost" from "Total Selling Price" and compare the remainder with the total in the column headed "Total Cash Investment" (column #7). Beware of one thing. The excess of "Total Selling Price" over "Total Cost" of properties can be represented by mortgages taken back on sale (column #3)—gain that won't be realized until mortgages are paid off, and not as good as cash. If "Cash Received At Sale" (column #2) is about equal to "Total Cash Investment" of each individual property, most of the gain on equity is represented by notes.

TABLE V
SALES OF PROPERTIES IN PRIOR PUBLIC PROGRAMS

Partnership/Property	Date Acquired	Date of Sale	(1) Mortgage Balance At Time Of Sale	(2) Cash Received At Sale*	(3) Notes Received At Sale	(4) Total Cash And Equity In Notes Received (2)+(3)	(5) Total Selling Price* (1)+(4)	Original Cost of Properties		
								(6) Original Mortgage Balance	(7) Total Cash Investment**	(8) Total Cost (6)+(7)
Public Partners II:										
Ewing Office Plaza—Dallas, Texas	8/21/73	10/14/77	$ 3,446	$ 238	$ 900	$ 1,138	$ 4,584	$ 3,531	$ 1,031	$ 4,562
Sea Pines Apartments—Charlotte, North Carolina	9/30/73	1/13/78	3,393	1,485	0	1,485	4,878	3,507	867	4,374
Boulevard Shopping Center—Buffalo, NY	11/14/73	3/06/78	19,783	7,905	2,250	10,155	29,938	19,222	4,433	23,655
Plantation Apartments—Atlanta, Georgia	11/21/73	9/10/78	3,350	235	565	800	4,150	3,400	991	4,391
Community Shopping Center—St. Louis, Missouri	12/18/73	8/21/79	2,359	191	416	607	2,966	2,199	657	2,856
Citizens Bank Building—Tampa, Florida	1/30/74	10/26/79	4,702	1,424	1,798	3,222	7,924	4,850	2,237	7,087
Pleasant Village Apartments—Austin, Texas	2/01/74	11/14/79	3,675	1,279	2,650	3,929	7,604	3,900	1,206	5,106
The Baker Building—New Orleans, Louisiana	3/30/74	3/05/80	1,195	254	1,205	1,459	2,654	1,537	555	2,092
			$41,903	$13,011	$9,784	$22,795	$64,698	$42,146	$11,977	$54,123

*Net of closing costs.
**Includes acquisition costs, capital improvements and closing costs.

STANGER PERFORMANCE SCHEDULES

If you're willing to take the time, you can compile a standardized track record using the method described below. Most of the information can be found in the offering document or in the audited annual reports for partnerships. Certain material is rearranged and numerous calculations are proposed to define prior performance. Inasmuch as sponsors are trying to get your business, we suggest you ask them to provide the material to you, so you may have a sensible and useful record of prior performance. Using standard information schedules for all sponsors will allow you to make valid comparisons between sponsors and come to conclusions on the issues of track record and relative performance. In addition, the schedules will enable you to organize the information you receive on your investments and quickly judge how well they are performing.

The methodology involves a two-step process. First, you need to complete the Performance Schedules for each of the sponsor's prior partnerships. These reporting forms help you assemble detailed and standardized performance profiles unavailable in present reports and prospectuses. (A complete set of Schedules and Instructions is provided at the end of this chapter.)

Once you have compiled information on property operations and partnership economic results on these standardized forms, you can then judge performance for specific properties, individual partnerships, partnership series and sponsors. The aggregate information for large numbers of properties, partnerships and sponsors will produce average performance figures which can act as a standard measure of average return. Such performance statistics will serve as a standard when you compare the performance of an individual property, partnership or sponsor.

The Performance Schedules present a standardized format for recording information on individual partnerships. The information captured focuses on Partnership Formation, Partnership Property Purchases, Property Sales, Partnership Operations, Partnership Economic Results Net to the Limited Partner, and Partnership Economic Results Including Market Value of Assets Net to the Limited Partner.

The Schedules can be used for public or private partnerships. By aggregating the results for all the partnerships offered by a sponsor, you will obtain a picture of composite performance.

Here is a summary of each schedule and how you can use the information captured.

Schedule A: Partnership Formation enables you to fix the precise amount and timing of real estate investments (a necessary step to evaluate performance) and judge the partnership's performance relative to its stated investment objectives. The Schedule summarizes the investment objectives of the partnership, shows front-end costs paid and the degree of leverage (an important risk factor), and gives a snapshot of the total amount of real estate working for you relative to your original investment.

With this information you can determine the average investment per property, the front-end cost percentage, the amount of cash investment in properties, and the total cost of the investment.

The details for all properties purchased by the partnership appear on **Schedule B: Partnership Property Purchases.** With this information you can evaluate the purchase price relative to the physical assets acquired (i.e., the number of rentable units, the square footage, and the type of property). You also can identify and group properties to compare purchase prices and performance based on location and property type.

In addition, financing information is provided so that the performance of each property and class of property can be evaluated based on the equity purchase price, the fully weighted cost of the property to the limited partners and the total purchase price (including mortgage debt). The purchase date fixes the precise holding period to calculate return on the asset purchase price when the property is sold. With this information and the data in Schedule C you can judge property performance based on the equity purchase price, the fully weighted cost (including a pro rata allocation of front-end costs) of the property to the limited partners, and the total purchase price (including mortgage debt).

Appreciation is the most important factor influencing your return from most real estate investments. Only when properties are sold do you find out exactly how well the sponsor has performed in selecting and managing your investment. **Schedule C: Property Sales** helps you track the management's actual record in selling properties. You can look at the difference between the purchase price of the property (as recorded in Schedule B) and the selling price and evaluate the appreciation on purchase price on a per annum basis.

In the tight mortgage markets of the last ten years, sellers of property generally took notes back to help purchasers buy property. When notes are taken back on the sale of partnership properties at below prevailing market rates, their actual economic value is below the face value of the note. We present a discounting methodology (Exhibit 2 of Appendix II at the end of this chapter) to use when adjusting the value of notes for interest rate differences—a necessary step to calculate actual economic returns on equity.

The information in Schedule C reflects property gain to the partnership rather than to the limited partner. While limited partner returns on sale are desirable to compute, at any given point in time they may be misleading. The reason: General partner participation in sales proceeds cannot be allocated to individual properties in an objective way. As the partnership liquidates more properties and the subordination provisions are achieved, the general partner will realize his incentive fee on aggregate property sales proceeds. The problem is how to allocate these fees back to properties sold and how to account for the disparity in reported general partner participation due solely to differing states of liquidation among partnerships. The solution is to judge property performance based on partnership returns on sale.

Schedule D: Partnership Operations establishes the current economic viability of the properties held by the partnership and gauges how well they are performing over time. You want to see improving results. Operating performance data should be aggregated and recorded annually for all properties and for each type of property held by the partnership, i.e., strip and enclosed mall shopping centers, urban and suburban office buildings, garden apartments, etc.

This schedule shows an operating record on the cash basis— the method of presentation knowledgeable real estate investors use. Maintaining a cash basis accounting record for all properties held by the partnership allows you to track operating cash flow before debt service, cash-on-cash returns based on total investment in the properties and other important property performance measures. Unfortunately, most partnerships are on an accrual basis of accounting. The sponsor may have to cooperate to provide this information. Operating information can be aggregated by property type and for the entire partnership portfolio. If you have the patience to stick with it, over time you will accumulate a valuable library of performance histories by which to judge the relative performance of various types of property investments and partnerships operated by the sponsor.

Return in a real estate investment is derived from three sources—tax savings, cash distributions from the property's net operating income, and appreciation when the property is sold. **Schedule E: Partnership Economic Results Net to Limited Partner** draws together annual operating results and property sale results to give you a picture of overall investment performance by the partnership to date.

Schedule E helps you judge how well an investment is doing in providing a competitive current yield on average investment. The time required for the partnership to pay back initial investment can be determined, and you can figure out the actual dollar amount of return realized so far. You can evaluate how tax savings, cash from operations and property sales proceeds have contributed to total return.

The difficulty in evaluating performance before all properties are liquidated is that interim property appreciation information is only available by appraisal. Sponsors are beginning to recognize the problem that investors want some indication of performance along the way, and more sponsors are providing appraisals of properties held. But, since most sponsors do not provide appraisal information, the "Adjusted Annual Return" method of analysis is the most appropriate measure of return available.

The concepts behind "Adjusted Annual Return" are: (1) distributions from sale and refinancing proceeds represent return of investment; (2) investment equals the average of the annual adjusted investment amounts (original investment reduced by sale and refinancing distributions); (3) all other returns (annual cash flow from operations, tax savings or costs, and distributions from sale and refinancing in excess of original investment) constitute return on investment. A standard internal rate-of-return calculation at the liquidation of a partnership results in almost exactly the same rate of return as the Adjusted Annual Return calculation.

During the period when the original investment is being paid back, the Adjusted Annual Return tends to approximate the cash distributions plus tax savings divided by original investment. After the investor has recouped his initial investment, the return increases with additional property sales and distribution of proceeds. The Adjusted Annual Return method is novel and frankly not ideal. But, it can be calculated with publicly available information. Until appraised values are provided by sponsors, Adjusted Annual Return is a useful approach.

"Realized Adjusted Annual Return" deals with cash distributions—one way to see the economics of the investment. However, distributing cash from initial working capital reserves (rather than real estate income) can influence the return rate and can give a false economic picture. Also, cash generated through operations or property sales may be retained as additional reserves. For these reasons, we present "Adjusted Annual Return" in Schedule E which includes cash distributions plus the partnership's net working capital.

The best method of calculating return includes the value of the assets remaining unsold in the portfolio. While there are significant problems in obtaining uniform appraisal values, the benefit to the investing public in analysis of prior performance far outweighs the cost, questions of comparability and the difficulties of providing property appraisals.

Schedule F: Partnership Economic Results Net to Limited Partners (Market Value Basis) incorporates the value of unsold partnership properties into the return analysis for those sponsors who supply appraisals of properties held, or "market value" balance sheets. The Schedule shows how to calculate rates of return using the Adjusted Annual Return, Percent Payback and Internal Rate of Return methods. You'll also see the impact of incentive fee arrangements with the general partner.

Schedule G: Summary Schedule draws together essential measures of return from the other Schedules to provide a composite picture of partnership performance. Results for property sales and for current operations indicate the appreciation realized on liquidated properties and the economic strength of properties still held by the partnership. Summary measures of return from operations reflect the sponsor's management skill and the economic strength of properties still held by the partnership. You want to track changes in these returns over time. Returns actually received by the investor ("Realized") and returns from undistributed cash and reserves, or unrealized appreciation ("Implied"), are summarized.

The appendices to this chapter explain additional analysis you can perform using the standardized Schedules and provide blank Schedules and detailed instructions. Additional Schedules (with more writing room!) are available from Robert A. Stanger & Co.

APPENDIX I: ADDITIONAL ANALYSIS

Additional calculations and how to make them using information in the Schedules are presented below.

Schedule A

1. Average Investment Per Property—Total Investment divided by Number of Properties. Amount Raised divided by Number of Properties.

2. Front-end Cost Percentage—the sum of Selling Commissions, Organization Expenses, Acquisition Fees and Acquisition Costs divided by (a) Amount Raised and/or (b) Total Investment.

3. Percentage Mortgage Leverage—Mortgage and Other Financing divided by Total Investment.

Schedule B

1. Unit Property Cost—Total Purchase Price divided by No. of Rentable Units or Square Feet. Be sure to adjust this figure to reflect the partnership's percentage ownership interest in the property.

2. Mortgage Financing Percentage—Mortgage Financing divided by Total Purchase Price.

Schedule C

1. Cash Percentage on Sale—Cash Down divided by the sum of Cash Down and Equity in Notes-Disc.

2. Annual Gain on Equity—Net Sale Proceeds to Partnership divided by Holding Period in Mos. times 12.

3. Annual Gain plus Aggregate Cash Flow—Net Sale Proceeds plus Aggregate Cash Flow divided by Holding Period in Mos. times 12.

4. Percent of Investment Returned Through Sales—(a) Net Sale Proceeds to Partnership divided by LP Cash Investment-Total (Schedule B), or (b) Net Sale Proceeds to Partnership plus Aggregate Cash Flow divided by LP Cash Investment-Total (Schedule B).

Schedule D

1. Gross Rent Multiplier—Total Purchase Price divided by Gross Revenues.

2. Trend Analysis—Compare Gross Revenues, Operating Expenses, Net Operating Income and Cash Generated with previous years. Compare Free-and-Clear Rate of Return and Cash-on-Cash Rate of Return with previous years.

Schedule E

1. Partitioning Return—Calculate the percentage of Total Economic Benefits or Cumulative Economic Benefits attributable to Tax Savings (Cost), Operating Cash Distributions, Cash Distributions from Reserves and Distributions from Sale/Refinancing.

2. Return on Your Investment—Multiply your cash investment in limited partnership interests by Realized Adjusted Annual Return, Realized Percent Payback of Original Investment, Adjusted Annual Return and Percent Payback of Original Investment.

Schedule F

1. Partitioning Return—Compare LP Participation in Net Worth with Total Return to see how much is attributable to unrealized appreciation.

2. Return on Your Actual Cash Investment in the Partnership—Multiply your cash investment in limited partnership interests by Adjusted Annual Return and Percent Payback of Original Investment.

3. Cost of Liquidation Fees—Divide GP Participation in Net Worth by the sum of GP Participation in Net Worth and LP Participation in Net Worth.

Summary Schedule

Information from the other schedules is summarized as to Operations, Property Sales and Economic Results Net to the Limited Partner.

APPENDIX II: SCHEDULES & INSTRUCTIONS

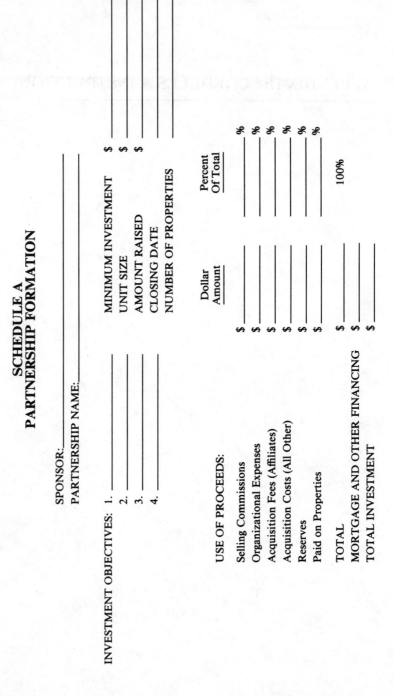

SCHEDULE A
PARTNERSHIP FORMATION

SPONSOR: _____

PARTNERSHIP NAME: _____

INVESTMENT OBJECTIVES:
1. _____
2. _____
3. _____
4. _____

MINIMUM INVESTMENT $ _____
UNIT SIZE $ _____
AMOUNT RAISED $ _____
CLOSING DATE   _____
NUMBER OF PROPERTIES   _____

USE OF PROCEEDS:

	Dollar Amount	Percent Of Total
Selling Commissions	$ _____	_____ %
Organizational Expenses	$ _____	_____ %
Acquisition Fees (Affiliates)	$ _____	_____ %
Acquisition Costs (All Other)	$ _____	_____ %
Reserves	$ _____	_____ %
Paid on Properties	$ _____	_____ %
TOTAL	$ _____	100%
MORTGAGE AND OTHER FINANCING	$ _____	
TOTAL INVESTMENT	$ _____	

SCHEDULE B
PARTNERSHIP PROPERTY PURCHASES

SPONSOR: _____

PARTNERSHIP NAME: _____

Property Name (1)	Type (2)	No. of Rentable Units/Sq. Ft. (3)	Location* (4)	Mo. & Yr. Purchased (5)	LP Cash Investment Acquisition Costs (6a)	LP Cash Investment Formation Costs (6b)	LP Cash Investment Total (6c)	Mortgage Financing (7)	Total Purchase Price (8)	Subsequent Additional Investments (9)
1.					$	$	$	$	$	$
2.										
3.										
4.										
5.										
6.										
7.										
8.										
9.										
10.										
11.										
12.										

*Refer to map (Exhibit 1) to identify location by one of six regional areas.

211

SCHEDULE C—PART 1
PARTNERSHIP PROPERTY SALES

(All sales prior to _____)

(Date)

SPONSOR: _____

PARTNERSHIP NAME: _____

Property Name	Mo. & Yr. Sold	Holding Period In Mos.	Gross Sale Proceeds				Expenses of Sale	GP Commission on Sale	Net Sale Proceeds to Others	
			Cash Down	Equity in Notes						
				Face	Disc.				Face	Disc.
(1)	(2)	(3)	(4a)	(4b)	(4c)		(5)	(6)	(7a)	(7b)
1.			$	$	$		$	$	$	$
2.										
3.										
4.										
5.										
6.										
7.										
8.										
9.										
10.										
11.										
12.										

SCHEDULE C—PART 2
PARTNERSHIP PROPERTY SALES

(All sales prior to _____)
(Date)

SPONSOR: _____

PARTNERSHIP NAME: _____

Property Name	Net Sale Proceeds to Partnership		LP Cash Investment (Total)	Gain on Sale		Annual Percent Appreciation On Equity		Aggregate Operating Cash Flow (Deficiency)	Annual Percent Return On Equity	
	Face	Disc.		Face	Disc.	Face	Disc.		Face	Disc.
	(8a)	(8b)	(9)	(10a)	(10b)	(11a)	(11b)	(12)	(13a)	(13b)
1.	$	$	$	$	$	%	%	$	%	%
2.										
3.										
4.										
5.										
6.										
7.										
8.										
9.										
10.										
11.										
12.										

213

SCHEDULE D—PART 1
PARTNERSHIP OPERATIONS (YEARS 1-4)

(Cash Basis)

SPONSOR: _____

PARTNERSHIP NAME: _____

PROPERTY GROUP: _____

(Indicate type of properties for which operating results are aggregated.)

	Year 1 (Date)	Year 2 (Date)	Year 3 (Date)	Year 4 (Date)
OPERATIONS (1):				
1. Gross Revenues	$	$	$	$
2. Operating Expenses	–	–	–	–
3. Net Operating Income	$	$	$	$
4. Debt Service	–	–	–	–
5. Cash Flow from Operations	$	$	$	$
6. Capital Additions	–	–	–	–
7. Due to Venture Partners	–	–	–	–
8. Cash Generated	$	$	$	$
INVESTMENT (2):				
9. LP Cash Investment—Acquisition	$	$	$	$
10. Additional Investment	+	+	+	+
11. Total Cash Investment	$	$	$	$
12. Mortgage Financing	+	+	+	+
13. Total Direct Property Investment	$	$	$	$
14. Free-and-Clear Rate of Return	%	%	%	%
15. Cash-on-Cash Rate of Return	%	%	%	%

(1) Not including proceeds or expenses of refinancing or sale.

(2) Only reflects Total Cash Investment and Mortgage Financing pro-rata for number of months owned during the year. Number of months owned divided by twelve (Pro-Rata Percentage) is multiplied by Total Cash Investment and Mortgage Financing (original principal amount) for each property.

SCHEDULE D—PART 2
PARTNERSHIP OPERATIONS (YEARS 5-8)

(Cash Basis)

SPONSOR: _____

PARTNERSHIP NAME: _____

PROPERTY GROUP: _____

(Indicate type of properties for which operating results are aggregated.)

	Year 5 (Date)	Year 6 (Date)	Year 7 (Date)	Year 8 (Date)
OPERATIONS (1):				
1. Gross Revenues	$	$	$	$
2. Operating Expenses	−	−	−	−
3. Net Operating Income	$	$	$	$
4. Debt Service	−	−	−	−
5. Cash Flow from Operations	$	$	$	$
6. Capital Additions	−	−	−	−
7. Due to Venture Partners	−	−	−	−
8. Cash Generated	$	$	$	$
INVESTMENT (2):				
9. LP Cash Investment—Acquisition	$	$	$	$
10. Additional Investment	+	+	+	+
11. Total Cash Investment	$	$	$	$
12. Mortgage Financing	+	+	+	+
13. Total Direct Property Investment	$	$	$	$
14. Free-and-Clear Rate of Return	%	%	%	%
15. Cash-on-Cash Rate of Return	%	%	%	%

(1) Not including proceeds or expenses of refinancing or sale.

(2) Only reflects Total Cash Investment and Mortgage Financing pro-rata for number of months owned during the year. Number of months owned divided by twelve (Pro-Rata Percentage) is multiplied by Total Cash Investment and Mortgage Financing (original principal amount) for each property.

215

SCHEDULE D—PART 3
PARTNERSHIP OPERATIONS (YEARS 9–12)

(Cash Basis)

SPONSOR: _____

PARTNERSHIP NAME: _____

PROPERTY GROUP: _____

(Indicate type of properties for which operating results are aggregated.)

	Year 9	Year 10	Year 11	Year 12
	(Date)	(Date)	(Date)	(Date)
OPERATIONS (1):				
1. Gross Revenues	$	$	$	$
2. Operating Expenses	−	−	−	−
3. Net Operating Income	$	$	$	$
4. Debt Service	−	−	−	−
5. Cash Flow from Operations	$	$	$	$
6. Capital Additions	−	−	−	−
7. Due to Venture Partners	−	−	−	−
8. Cash Generated	$	$	$	$
INVESTMENT (2):				
9. LP Cash Investment—Acquisition	$	$	$	$
10. Additional Investment	+	+	+	+
11. Total Cash Investment	$	$	$	$
12. Mortgage Financing	+	+	+	+
13. Total Direct Property Investment	$	$	$	$
14. Free-and-Clear Rate of Return	%	%	%	%
15. Cash-on-Cash Rate of Return	%	%	%	%

(1) Not including proceeds or expenses of refinancing or sale.

(2) Only reflects Total Cash Investment and Mortgage Financing pro-rata for number of months owned during the year. Number of months owned divided by twelve (Pro-Rata Percentage) is multiplied by Total Cash Investment and Mortgage Financing (original principal amount) for each property.

SCHEDULE E—PART 1
PARTNERSHIP ECONOMIC RESULTS NET TO LIMITED PARTNER

SPONSOR: _____

PARTNERSHIP NAME: _____

ORIGINAL INVESTMENT: $ _____

Year (1)	Ordinary Loss (Income) (2)	Capital Loss (Gain) (3)	Tax Savings (Cost) (4)	Operating Cash Distributions (5)	Cash Distributions From Reserves (6)	Distributions From Sale/Refinancing (7)	Total Economic Benefits (8)
	$	$	$	$	$	$	$

SCHEDULE E—PART 2
PARTNERSHIP ECONOMIC RESULTS NET TO LIMITED PARTNER

SPONSOR: _____

PARTNERSHIP NAME: _____

ORIGINAL INVESTMENT: $ _____

Year	Cumulative Distributions From Sale/Refinancing (9)	Cumulative Economic Benefits (10)	Adjusted Investment (11)	Cumulative Adjusted Investment (12)	Realized Adjusted Annual Return (13)	Realized Percent Payback Of Original Investment (14)
	$	$	$	$	%	%

SCHEDULE E—PART 3
PARTNERSHIP ECONOMIC RESULTS NET TO LIMITED PARTNER

SPONSOR: _____

PARTNERSHIP NAME: _____

ORIGINAL INVESTMENT: $ _____

Year	Cumulative Economic Benefits (15)	Partnership Net Working Capital (16)	Total Current Return (17)	Cumulative Adjusted Investment (18)	Adjusted Annual Return (19)	Percent Payback Of Original Investment (20)
	$	$	$	$	%	%

SCHEDULE F—PART 1
PARTNERSHIP ECONOMIC RESULTS NET TO LIMITED PARTNER
(Market Value Basis)

SPONSOR: _____

PARTNERSHIP NAME: _____

ORIGINAL INVESTMENT: $ _____

Year	Net Working Capital	Notes (Discounted)	Partnership Items Net Current Value Of Properties	Net Worth	GP Participation in Net Worth	LP Participation in Net Worth
(1)	(2a)	(2b)	(2c)	(2d)	(3)	(4)
	$	$	$	$	$	$

SCHEDULE F—PART 2
PARTNERSHIP ECONOMIC RESULTS NET TO LIMITED PARTNER

(Market Value Basis)

SPONSOR: _____

PARTNERSHIP NAME: _____

ORIGINAL INVESTMENT: $ _____

Year	Total Economic Benefits (5)	Cumulative Economic Benefits (6)	Total Return (7)	Cumulative Adjusted Investment (8)	Implied Adjusted Annual Return (9)	Implied Percent Payback of Original Investment (10)	Implied Internal Rate Of Return (11)
	$	$	$	$	%	%	%

SUMMARY SCHEDULE

SPONSOR: _____

PARTNERSHIP NAME: _____ FRONT-END COST PERCENTAGE: ____ %

ORIGINAL INVESTMENT: $ _____ LEVERAGE PERCENTAGE: ____ %

Economic Results Net to Limited Partner

	Operations		Property Sales		Realized Return		Implied Return		
Year	Free-and-Clear Rate of Return	Cash-on-Cash Rate of Return	Weighted Average Annual Percent Return on Equity	Percent of Portfolio Liquidated	Adjusted Annual Return	Percent Payback of Original Investment	Adjusted Annual Return	Percent Payback of Original Investment	Internal Rate of Return
(1)	(2)	(3)	(4)	(5)	(6)	(7)	(8)	(9)	(10)
	%	%	%	%	%	%	%	%	%

INSTRUCTIONS FOR THE SCHEDULES

All of the column headings in the Schedules are defined in the instructions that follow. Two attachments to the instructions are also included. Exhibit 1 is a map to define "Location" for Schedule B. Exhibit 2 is a description of the method to discount the value of notes taken back on sale in Schedule C and Schedule F. In most cases we have tried to use terminology commonly found in prospectuses. We believe you can fill in most of the columns from prospectus information and from annual reports for Schedules A and B. In Schedules C, D, E and F certain information must be provided by the sponsor. These items are indicated below by an asterisk. The instructions below are identified by schedule and column number for easy reference.

These Schedules are set up to record aggregate partnership results and not results per unit of investment. Aggregate results provide data applicable to all investors regardless of the size of their investment. In order to translate to your investment, multiply percentages developed (such as cash-on-cash return, rate of return, average annual return, or payback of original investment) by the amount of your investment.

Schedule A: Partnership Information

Self-explanatory.

Schedule B: Property Purchases

1. **Property Name**—Identification.

2. **Type**—Group and list by category (i.e., apartment, shopping center, office building, subsidized housing, commercial net lease, hotel, mini-warehouse, industrial, other).

3. **Number of Rentable Units or Square Feet**—self-explanatory.

4. **Location**—Indicate region (see map attached as Exhibit 1).

5. **Mo. & Yr. Purchased**—Indicate month and year purchase

was closed (first payment made to seller other than for an option).

6. **L.P. Cash Investment**
   a. **Acquisition Costs**—Include cash paid to sellers, acquisition fees to all parties, and other property acquisition fees and expenses.
   b. **Formation Costs**—Pro rata underwriting commissions and organization expenses based on acquisition cost percentages (acquisition cost of a property divided by acquisition costs of all properties, times total partnership formation costs).
   c. **Total**—Acquisition Costs plus Formation Costs, plus Additional Investment.

7. **Mortgage Financing**—Aggregate principal amount of mortgages assumed or granted at time of purchase.

8. **Total Purchase Price**—Total LP Cash Investment plus Mortgage Financing.

9. **Subsequent Additional Investments**—Subsequent investment, such as balloon amortization payments, buyouts of venture partners, capital additions and others.

Schedule C.: Partnership Property Sales

(All sales prior to _____ .)
                          (date)

1. **Property Name**—Same as Schedule B.

2. **Mo. and Yr. Sold**—Month and year property was sold.

3. **Holding Period in Months**—Number of months property was owned. Mo. and Yr. Purchased (Schedule B) compared to Mo. and Yr. Sold.

4. **Gross Sale Proceeds**—Amount available to Partnership from proceeds of sale in cash or notes.
   a. **Cash Down**—Net cash from sale proceeds.
   b. **Equity in Notes**—Notes (Face Value) received on sale at par value gross to the Partnership.
   c. **Equity in Notes—Disc.***—Discounted value of notes

received on sale gross to the partnership. See Exhibit 2 for method of discounting to present value.

5. **Expenses of Sale**—Costs of sale paid to unaffiliated third parties.

6. **GP Commission on Sale**—Sale proceeds paid or payable to GP as commission on sale.

7. **Net Sale Proceeds to Others**
   a. **Face**—Gross sale proceeds (based on face value of notes received as proceeds from sale) paid or payable to others.
   b. **Disc.***—Gross sale proceeds (based on discounted value of notes received on sale) paid or payable to others.

8. **Net Sale Proceeds to Partnership**
   a. **Face**—Gross Sale Proceeds (based on face value of notes received on sale) less Expenses of Sale, less GP Commission on Sale and less Net Sale Proceeds to Others—Face.
   b. **Disc.**—Gross Sale Proceeds (based on discounted value of notes received on sale) less Expenses of Sale, less GP Commission on Sale and less Net Sale Proceeds to Others-Disc.

9. **LP Cash Investment (Total)**—Schedule B, column #6c.

10. **Gain on Sale**
    a. **Face**—Net Sale Proceeds to Partnership—Face less LP Cash Investment—Total and less Subsequent Additional Investment from Schedule B, column #9.
    b. **Disc.**—Net Sale Proceeds to Partnership-Disc. less LP Cash Investment—Total and less subsequent Additional Investment from Schedule B, column #9.

11. **Annual Percent Appreciation on Equity (Face Value or Disc.)**—Gain on Sale (either Face Value or Disc.), divided by LP Cash Investment-Total gives Percentage Gain on Sale. Divide Percentage Gain on Sale by number of years

property was held to calculate Annual Percent Appreciation on Equity. (Holding period in months divided by 12 will give number of years property was held. Use fractional year.)

12. **Aggregate Operating Cash Flow (Deficiency)**—Cumulative net operating cash flow or loss during holding period net of capital additions.

13. **Annual Percent Return on Equity (Face Value or Disc.)**—Gain on Sale (either Face or Disc.) plus Aggregate Operating Cash Flow (Deficiency) gives "Return on Equity." "Percent Return on Equity" is Return on Equity divided by LP Cash Investment-Total. Divide Percent Return on Equity by number of years property was held to calculate Annual Percent Return on Equity. (Holding period in months divided by 12 will give number of years property was held. Use fractional years.)

Schedule D: Partnership Operations (Cash Basis)*

Note: Operating performance data can be aggregated annually for each type of property held by the partnership and recorded on separate Schedules. For example, operating data for all urban office buildings held by the partnership can be aggregated and recorded separately from data for garden apartment properties. Also, operating data for all partnership properties can be recorded on Schedule D. The entries on this schedule are the sum of Schedule D lines #1 through #13 for all other property groups. Lines #14 and #15 should then be recomputed from the aggregated data.

1. **Gross Revenues**—Rents, interest and other income.

2. **Operating Expenses**—All property operating expenses plus replacement reserves, insurance, taxes, ground rent. Does not include partnership operating expenses.

3. **Net Operating Income**—Gross Revenues minus Operating Expenses.

4. **Debt Service**—The annual total of interest and principal on all indebtedness on the property.

5. **Cash Flow From Operations**—Net Operating Income less Debt Service.

6. **Capital Additions**—Capitalized expenditures on properties, such as additions, betterments, and replacements.

7. **Due to Venture Partners**—Amounts payable to sellers or venturers from Cash Flow From Operations less Capital Additions.

8. **Cash Generated**—Cash Flow from Operations less Capital Additions and less amounts Due to Venture Partners.

Note: #9, 10 & 11 as defined below must be multiplied by Pro Rata Percentage to reflect the number of months the property was owned during the year. Pro Rata Percentage equals the number of months owned during the year divided by twelve.

9. **L.P. Cash Investment—Acquisition**—Sum total of column #6a—Schedule B amounts for each property owned for any portion of the year.

10. **Additional Investment**—Subsequent investment, such as balloon payments and buyouts of venture partners and others from Schedule B.

11. **Total Cash Investment**—LP Cash Investment—Acquisition Cost plus Additional Investment.

12. **Mortgage Financing**—Original principal amount of all mortgages, subsequent financings and liens to which properties are subject.

13. **Total Direct Property Investment**—Total Cash Investment plus Mortgage Financing.

14. **Free-and-Clear Rate Of Return**—Net Operating Income divided by Total Direct Property Investment.

15. **Cash-on-Cash Rate Of Return**—Cash Generated divided by Total Cash Investment.

Schedule E: Partnership Economic Results Net to Limited Partner

1. **Year**—Self-explanatory.

2. **Ordinary Loss (Income)**—LP's allocable share of ordinary income or loss.

3. **Capital Loss (Gain)**—LP's allocable share of net capital gain or loss.

4. **Tax Savings (Cost)**—.5 (or applicable income tax bracket) times Ordinary Loss (Income) plus .2 (or applicable capital gain tax bracket) times Capital Loss (Gain). (For pre-1979 capital loss (gain), multiply by .25.)

5. **Operating Cash Distributions**—LP's allocable share of total cash distributions less the sum of Cash Distributions from Reserves and Distributions from Sale/Refinancing.

6. **Cash Distributions From Reserves**—LP's allocable share of Cash Distributions from Reserves.

7. **Distributions From Sale/Refinancing**—LP's allocable share of cash distributions of proceeds from the sale or refinancing of partnership properties.

8. **Total Economic Benefits**—Tax Savings (Cost) plus Operating Cash Distributions, Cash Distributions from Reserves, and Distributions from Sale/Refinancing.

9. **Cumulative Distributions From Sale/Refinancing**—The sum of Distributions from Sale/Refinancing for all years of Partnership operations.

10. **Cumulative Economic Benefits**—The sum of Total Economic Benefits for all years of Partnership operations.

11. **Adjusted Investment**—Use of Proceeds-Total from Schedule A less one-half the sum of current-year and prior-year Cumulative Distributions From Sale/Refinancing. In the first year, Adjusted Investment should be pro-rated to

reflect the number of months between partnership Closing Date (Schedule A) and year end. Multiply Use of Proceeds-Total by the number of months between Closing Date and year end divided by twelve. When Cumulative Distributions from Sale/Refinancing exceed Original Investment, let Adjusted Investment equal zero.

12. **Cumulative Adjusted Investment**—The sum of Adjusted Investment for all years of partnership operation.

13. **Realized Adjusted Annual Return**—Cumulative Economic Benefits less Cumulative Distributions from Sale/Refinancing (not to exceed Use of Proceeds-Total) divided by Cumulative Adjusted Investment.

14. **Realized Percent Payback of Original Investment**—Cumulative Economic Benefits divided by Use of Proceeds-Total from Schedule A.

15. **Cumulative Economic Benefits**—from column #10.

16. **Partnerhip Net Working Capital**—The excess of Partnership current assets (reduced by the current amount of notes receivable) over current liabilities (reduced by the current amount of mortgages payable) according to generally accepted accounting principles.

17. **Total Current Return**—The sum of Cumulative Economic Benefits and Partnership Net Working Capital.

18. **Cumulative Adjusted Investment**—from column #12.

19. **Adjusted Annual Return**—Total Current Return less Cumulative Distributions from Sale/Refinancing (not to exceed Use of Proceeds-Total) divided by Cumulative Adjusted Investment.

20. **Percent Payback of Original Investment** — Total Current Return divided by Use of Proceeds-Total from Schedule A.

Schedule F: Partnership Economic Results Net to Limited Partner (Market Value Basis)

1. **Year**—Self-explanatory.
2. **Partnership Items**
   a. **Net Working Capital**—Excess of Partnership current assets over current liabilities according to generally accepted accounting principles.
   b. **Notes (Discounted)***—Present value (as of current year-end) of outstanding notes taken back on sales of partnership property discounted according to the method in Exhibit 2.
   c. **Net Current Value of Properties**—Appraised value of partnership properties as of current year-end less outstanding debt, estimated costs of sale and share due venture partners.
   d. **Net Worth***—The sum of Net Working Capital, Notes (Discounted), and Net Current Value of Properties, or the reported net worth if a market value balance sheet is available.

3. **GP Participation in Net Worth***—The general partner's share of Net Worth.

4. **LP Participation in Net Worth**—Partnership Net Worth less GP Participation in Net Worth.

5. **Total Economic Benefits**—From Schedule E.

6. **Cumulative Economic Benefits**—From Schedule E.

7. **Total Return**—The sum of Cumulative Economic Benefits and LP Participation in Net Worth.

8. **Cumulative Adjusted Investment**—From Schedule E.

9. **Implied Adjusted Annual Return**—Total Return less Cumulative Distributions from Sale/Refinancing from Schedule E (not to exceed Use of Proceeds Total) divided by Cumulative Adjusted Investment.

10. **Implied Percent Payback of Original Investment**—Total Return divided by Use of Proceeds—Total from Schedule A.

11. **Implied Internal Rate of Return**—The discount rate which equates each year's Total Economic Benefits and the current year's LP Participation in Net Worth with the Original Investment.

Summary Schedule

1. **Year**—self-explanatory.

2. **Free-and-Clear Rate of Return**—Schedule D (All Partnership Properties), line 14 for current year.

3. **Cash-on-Cash Rate of Return**—Schedule D (All Partnership Properties), line 15 for current year.

4. **Weighted Average Annual Percent Return on Equity**—(a) Multiply Annual Percent Return on Equity-Disc. (Schedule C, column #13b) by LP Cash Investment-Total (Schedule C, column #9) for each property sold and sum the amounts. (b) Sum LP Cash Investment-Total (Schedule C, column #9) for all properties sold. (c) Divide (a) by (b).

5. **Percent of Portfolio Liquidated**—Add LP Cash Investment-Total (Schedule B, column #6c) and Subsequent Additional Investment (Schedule B, column #9) for all properties sold. Divide by the sum of Amount Raised (Schedule A) and the total of all Subsequent Additional Investment (Schedule B, column #9).

6. **Realized Adjusted Annual Return**—Schedule E, column #13.

7. **Realized Percent Payback of Original Investment**—Schedule E, column #14.

8. **Implied Adjusted Annual Return**—Schedule F, column #9.

9. **Implied Percent Payback of Original Investment**—Schedule F, column #10.

10. **Implied Internal Rate of Return**—Schedule F, column #11.

*Indicates information which usually must be provided by the sponsor.

EXHIBIT 1

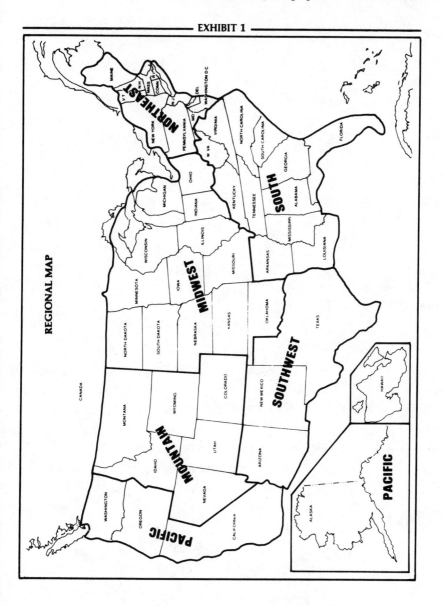

EXHIBIT 2: DISCOUNTING METHODOLOGY

When partnerships sell properties, purchase mortgage notes can be taken back as part of the sales price. The interest rate on these notes may be lower than the market rate prevailing at the time of sale. In such cases, the actual economic value of the notes taken back is less than the face value, and property sale prices are correspondingly lower. The discounting method to adjust for notes taken back on sale is explained below.

DISCOUNTING NOTES FOR SCHEDULE C— PROPERTY SALES

Follow these steps:

(1) Standardize the note payment schedules on a quarterly basis beginning with the date of sale. In the case of a wraparound note held by the partnership, deduct both principal and interest payments on the underlying debt from the gross payments on the wraparound note to determine the quarterly payments on the net equity in the note. In the case where additional interest is accrued, this additional interest should not be included in the payment schedule until paid.

(2) Calculate the discounted present value of note payments receivable as of the sale date. Discount the series of quarterly payments resulting from Step 1, including any balloon payments receivable. Use a quarterly discounting method and the

discount rate prevailing during the year of sale as indicated in the table below.

The value so derived represents a reasonable estimate of the economic value of the note at the time of property sale. This figure should be recorded in Schedule C, column #4c.

DISCOUNTING NOTES FOR SCHEDULE F

The method is the same as indicated for Schedule C. However, use only the equity remaining in the notes as of the date of evaluation—i.e., the receivable portion of the remaining scheduled payments. The discount factor applied should be the discount rate (see following table) for the most recent year end. (For Schedule C, the discount rate used is the discount rate prevailing in the year of sale.) Record the result of this calculation on Schedule F, column #2b.

DISCOUNT RATES FOR PROPERTY SALES ANALYSIS

Year	6-Month Treasury Bills (%)	Discount Rates (%)
1984	9.76	12.69
1983	8.73	11.35
1982	11.08	14.41
1981	13.81	18.00
1980	11.37	14.81
1979	10.01	13.04
1978	7.57	9.86
1977	5.51	7.18
1976	5.26	6.85
1975	6.12	7.97
1974	7.92	10.32
1973	7.17	9.34
1972	4.46	5.81
1971	4.51	5.87
1970	6.56	8.55
1969	6.85	8.92
1968	5.47	7.12

NOTE: The above discount rates are derived by taking 130% of the average 6-month Treasury Bill rate as reported in the Federal Reserve Bulletin for the corresponding period.

SECTION V

EVALUATING
PARTNERSHIP PROGRESS

CHAPTER 24

TRACKING PRIOR INVESTMENTS

Up to this point, we've presented evaluation techniques to guide your selection of a real estate partnership investment. After making the initial investment decision, you need a way to track partnership progress and know where you stand at any point in time.

Unfortunately, one of the biggest problems facing real estate partnership investors today is knowing how well their investment is performing. The reason: Historic cost financial statements for real estate companies are based on depreciating property and are misleading. Depreciation reduces book value, or stated net worth, and artificially reduces taxable earnings. But, with good management and good luck, property will appreciate. For real estate companies, this hoped-for result is not portrayed in financial statements assembled according to generally accepted accounting principles ("GAAP").

Holders of illiquid, long-term partnership investments would like to have their "faith" bolstered with some tangible evidence of prosperity. Unlike stocks, partnership values cannot be found in the daily newspaper. Instead, investors rely on the financial reports and communications provided by the sponsor. Most sponsors of publicly registered real estate limited partnerships fulfill only the minimum financial reporting requirements of the Securities and Exchange Commission for informing investors about financial results. (Private placement reporting is often even more sparse.) Usually, details include the business of the partnership, summary financial data and a management discussion and analysis of financial condition and operations. In addition, to comply with disclosure requirements, the general partner must show amounts paid to the sponsor and affiliates. Most sponsors provide a table showing a summary of cash distributions and, sometimes, tax loss. Sponsors typically provide a limited description of events during the year, specifically referencing properties acquired or sold and cash distributions.

The information provided is a good start but falls far short of giving investors what they need to tell where they stand. For instance, financial statements of multi-property public partnerships usually are not restated to reflect discontinued operations (properties sold). So, if the statement you examine is one in which a significant number of properties are sold (or bought, for that matter) during the year, you can't draw conclusions about the trend of operations and the level of property values.

The standard reporting format does not include management's estimate of the property values in the portfolio or show financial statements on a market value basis. So-called "fair market value" financial reporting is required for larger real estate companies in corporate and trust form but is not required for partnerships.

Usually, sponsors do not even provide comparisons of operations with prior periods, either for the entire property portfolio or for segments (which would be more revealing), such as apartments, shopping centers, etc. If you were given this information, you could see the trend of rents, net operating income, cash flow and expenses, and you could quickly identify superior or inferior performance.

But, if you look at the sparse reported financial information in certain ways, you still can get a rough idea of property values. True, the method is not ideal, but it works both for private and public offering financial statements. Here's how to do it.

THE METHOD

THE METHOD

Start by removing all property assets and mortgage liabilities to derive "Adjusted Balance Sheet Items" net of real estate items. Then, use the concept of "capitalization rate." Take rental income and subtract property operating expense. The result is net operating income ("NOI"). Multiply NOI times twelve (an 8.5% capitalization rate) to figure an approximate Market Value of Real Estate assets. Then, subtract the mortgage debt to give Net Real Estate Value.

Add the Adjusted Balance Sheet Items to the Net Real Estate Value. Compare this total, called Equity Value, to the total original limited partnership capital contributions to see how the investment stands overall. If you simply compare Market Value of Real Estate to original investment in land and buildings, you can see the appreciation on the property's purchase price.

For the purpose of demonstrating how to use the method, let's look at two sample annual reports. Partnership A raised $12 million in limited partner capital contributions; Partnership B raised about $60 million. Both partnerships have four years of operating history. In Partnership B, certain properties have been sold, whereas no properties have been sold in Partnership A. The reason for selecting two partnerships: Reporting practices vary; by showing the methods for each, you should have the basis for understanding almost any partnership you look at.

EXAMPLE #1: No Property Sales During Report Period

Here's how to adjust the balance sheet for Partnership A (see Table I on the next page). Total Current Assets are $1.8 million. Ignore Investment Properties for now. Add Deferred Expenses and Deferred Loan Fees of $.4 million for Total Adjusted Assets of $2.2 million. (You are half way toward Adjusted Balance Sheet Items.)

Now, look at the liability side of the balance sheet. Notes Payable refers to property debt. The Partners' Equity section

TABLE I
PARTNERSHIP A
BALANCE SHEET

Assets	
Cash and cash equivalents	$ 1,769,000
Accounts receivable, net of allowance for doubtful accounts of $82,000	35.000
Deferred expenses and other assets, at cost	338,000
Deferred loan fee, at cost, net of accumulated amortization of $10,000	41,000
Investment properties, at cost, net of accumulated depreciation of $4,752,000	20,835,000
Total Assets	$23,018,000

Liabilities and Partners' Equity	
Liabilities:	
Notes payable, net of unamortized discounts of $2,869,000	$15,754,000
Accounts payable and accrued expenses	188,000
Accrued interest payable	74,000
Property taxes payable	471,000
General Partner management fee payable	—
Unearned rents and security deposits	252,000
Total Liabilities	$16,739,000
Partners' equity:	
Limited Partners' equity (12,000 Limited Partnership Units outstanding)	6,202,000
General Partners' equity	77,000
Total Partners' equity	$ 6,279,000
Total Liabilities and partners' equity	$23,018,000

shows partnership book net worth which is what we are recalculating. So, ignore Notes Payable and Partner's Equity for the time being because they are real estate items. Take all other items under Liabilities which equal $1.0 million. Subtract this amount of Adjusted Liabilities from the $2.2 million of Total Adjusted Assets to get Adjusted Balance Sheet Items of $1.2 million.

To calculate real estate value using the capitalization rate concept, start with Rental Income of $4.8 million (see Table II). Subtract Property Operating Expenses, Property Taxes and Repairs and Maintenance which total $1.9 million, leaving NOI of about $2.8 million. Ignore Interest Income as it represents earnings on current assets, not real estate. In the expense items, ignore Interest because debt is subtracted later to determine Net

TABLE II
PARTNERSHIP A
STATEMENT OF OPERATIONS

Revenues:	
Rental and other income	$4,756,000
Interest income	174,000
Total revenues	$4,930,000
Costs and expenses:	
Interest, including amortization of note discounts of $173,000	$1,787,000
Depreciation and amortization	1,361,000
Operating expenses—investment properties	1,071,000
Property taxes	517,000
Repairs and maintenance	331,000
Property management fees to affiliate	226,000
General Partner management fees	66,000
General and Administrative	42,000
Total costs and expenses	$5,401,000
Net Loss	$ 471,000

Real Estate Value. Depreciation is a noncash charge, an accounting fiction, so ignore it. And, General Partner Management Fees and General and Administrative costs aren't property operating expenses. They don't affect real estate value so ignore them too.

At a capitalization rate of 8.5%, the approximate Market Value of Real Estate is $34.0 million—$2.8 million of Net Operating Income times twelve. This value is described as "free and clear," meaning the property value is exclusive of, or before subtraction of, mortgage debt. Add back Unamortized Discount to Notes Payable in Table I (because if the properties were sold, the face amount of the Notes must be repaid). This equals $18.6 million. So, Net Real Estate Value is $15.4 million ($34.0 less $18.6). Add $1.2 million of Adjusted Balance Sheet Items for an approximate Equity Value of $16.6 million.

The difference between approximate Equity Value of $16.6 million and the original limited partner capital contribution of $12 million is unrealized appreciation of $4.6 million, or 38% on investment. The unrealized increase in Equity Value is $383 per $1,000 unit of investment.

243

Looking at appreciation from another perspective, start with approximate Market Value of Real Estate of $34.0 million. Then, figure original property cost by adding Investment Properties, ($20.8 million) and accumulated depreciation ($4.8 million), which equals the original cost of properties of $25.6 million. In less than four years, Market Value of Real Estate appreciated 33% from the original cost of properties ($34 million versus $25.6 million). (Appreciation on Equity Value is greater because of leverage.)

Cash distributions to limited partners since inception of partnership operations amounted to $2.2 million, or $185 per $1,000 invested. Accumulated tax loss is $2.5 million. (These items are included in the annual report.) So, tax savings (at 50%) are about $1.2 million or $102 a unit. Cash distributions plus tax savings total $3.4 million, or $287 per unit. Remaining Equity Value is $1,383 per unit. Total value of the investment to date is $1,670 ($185 + $102 + $1,383).

During the year of this report, the partnership was fully invested. No properties were either purchased or sold. Under these circumstances the rental income figure reflects operations of properties for a full year, and the capitalization rate methodology outlined is suitable to arrive at an approximation of possible property value.

EXAMPLE #2: Properties Sold During The Report Period

Partnership B's balance sheet and income statement reflect properties sold for a combination of cash and notes during the reporting year and in previous years. So, the analysis is more complicated than for Partnership A, although the same method works. (The analytical problems created by partially liquidated portfolios do not exist in single-property private placements.)

First, adjust the balance sheet (see Table III). The property accounts are presented first. Ignore this part for now. Look at the rest of the assets. A large entry, Notes Receivable ($28.7 million), represents notes taken back on sale of properties. The

TABLE III
PARTNERSHIP B
BALANCE SHEET

Assets

Property:	
Land	$ 9,727,000
Land improvements	6,715,000
Buildings	78,226,000
Furniture and fixtures.................................	10,323,000
	104,991,000
Less accumulated depreciation............................	(16,382,000)
	88,609,000
Cash	895,000
Government National Mortgage Association (GNMA) pass-through	
certificates, at cost (market value – $3,293,000)	3,776,000
Notes receivable (Note 1)................................	28,744,000
Other assets...	2,860,000
Total Assets...	$124,884,000

Liabilities and Partners' Capital (Deficit)

Notes payable (Note 1)....................................	$ 81,913,000
Accounts payable (including $142,000 payable to affiliates)........	596,000
Other Liabilities	3,144,000
Total Liabilities	85,653,000
Partners' capital (deficit):	
General Partners..	(30,000)
Limited Partners.......................................	39,261,000
Total Partners' Capital	39,231,000
Total Liabilities and Partners' Capital	$124,884,000

1. Notes receivable and payable at October 24, 1982 consist of the following:

	Notes Receivable	Notes Payable	Net Equity
Notes on sold properties	$41,650,000	$11,542,000	$30,108,000
Notes on owned properties		68,783,000	
Short-term loans		6,600,000	
	41,650,000	86,925,000	
Less: unamortized discounts	(11,427,000)	(5,012,000)	
deferred gain	(1,479,000)		
	$28,744,000	$81,913,000	

footnote indicates the value of the notes is discounted ("marked
to the market") because the interest rate on the note differed
from market rates prevailing when the notes were taken back.
No further adjustment is necessary. Add this discounted note

value to Cash, Securities and Other Assets. From Table III, total assets are $36.3 million, exclusive of real estate.

To figure Adjusted Liabilities, add Accounts Payable and Other Liabilities for a total of $3.7 million. The Notes Payable liability of $81.9 million includes $68.8 million of mortgages on properties owned which are ignored (subtracted) for now because we are not figuring real estate values yet. Of the remaining $13.1 million, Notes on Property Sold accounts for $11.5 million. The footnote indicates a $5.0 million adjustment to all Notes Payable for unamortized discount. Reduce Notes Payable on Properties Sold to $6.5. Other Notes Payable are for Short Term Loans ($6.6 million). Other Liabilities are $3.7 million, for total Adjusted Liabilities of $16.8 million ($13.1 plus $3.7). The Partners' Capital Account section of the balance sheet will be replaced with a new Equity Value figure after the real estate value calculations, so ignore it for now. The Adjusted Balance Sheet is $19.5 million ($36.3 of Adjusted Assets less $16.8 of Adjusted Liabilities).

For the capitalization rate calculation (see Table IV on the next page), Rental Income totaled $22.9 million. (The income item Gain on Sale is ignored here because the resulting values are represented in Notes Receivable and Cash or Securities on the balance sheet.) Property Operating Expense is separately broken out and includes Property Taxes ($1.7 million), Utilities ($2.7 million) and Property Operations ($8.4 million) for a total of $12.8 million. In the expense items, ignore Interest Income which relates to Notes Receivable, not property, partnership Administrative Cost, Depreciation and Interest Expense (the same as in the previous example because the debt amount is subtracted to determine Equity Value).

Property Net Operating Income of $10.1 million ($22.9 of Rental Income less $12.8 of Property Operating Expense) times twelve equals the approximate "free-and-clear" Market Value of Real Estate of $121.2 million. From this amount you subtract Notes on Owned Properties (mortgage debt) of $68.8 million (from footnote 1, Table III). Net Real Estate Value is

TABLE IV
PARTNERSHIP B
STATEMENT OF OPERATIONS

Income:	
Rental..	$22,916,000
Interest..	3,815,000
	26,731,000
Expenses:	
Administrative (including $217,000 in 1981 and $210,000 in 1980 to affiliates)	394,000
Depreciation	6,136,000
Interest and loan fees (including $6,000 in 1981 and $69,000 in 1979 to affiliates)...............................	9,774,000
Property taxes	1,707,000
Utilities	2,712,000
Property operations (including $3,987,000 to affiliates).......	8,391,000
	29,114,000
Loss before gain on sale of property and extraordinary item ..	(2,383,000)
Gain on sale of property.............................	5,496,000
Income (loss) before extraordinary item..................	3,113,000
Loss from early extinguishment of debt..................	—
Net income (loss)...................................	$ 3,113,000

$52.4. Then, add $19.5 of Adjusted Balance Sheet Items for an Equity Value of the partnership of $71.9.

Cumulative cash distributions to limited partners total $17.6 million. Tax savings equal $1.1 million. Total value of the investment to date (including unrealized gain) is $90.6 million ($71.9 + $17.6 + $1.1) compared to original limited partner capital contributions of approximately $60 million. On two units (representing $1,000 of investment) cash distributions equal $292, tax savings equal $18 and remaining Equity Value, including unrealized gain, amounts to $1,195. Total value of the investment to date is $1,505 ($292 + $18 + $1,195).

Approximately $38 million of properties at cost have been sold (from "Cost of Sale" in the financial statement footnotes) or about 27% of the portfolio at original cost. The good news: The gains are booked, even though only a portion are in cash. The bad news: Less property per dollar of original investment is left for future gains.

PROBLEMS

You have to read management's statement about operations for the year to pick up adjustment factors. One of the inaccuracies of the method arises when properties are sold during the year and rental income is not adjusted for discontinued operations. (This is only a problem in looking at multiple-property partnerships, not a single-property private placement.) Some of the value of these properties is counted twice, once in Capitalized Income and again in Cash or Notes Receivable. This factor caused an overstatement of value in the case of Partnership B because four properties costing $22 million were sold during 1982. The amount of overstatement could be as much as $10 to $20 million, or about $250 per $1,000 of investment. Total value of Partnership B should be adjusted downward for this factor.

Conversely, analyzing financial statements in a year during which property was acquired, Rental Income would not include a full year's results. But, Notes Payable on the balance sheet would include the full amount of the mortgage on the property. Property value would be unrealistically low.

Another problem is using the same capitalization rate for different kinds of property, because market capitalization rates vary. (Again, this is not a problem in single-property private placements.) In general, shopping centers are valued at the highest price (lowest capitalization rates). Office buildings are in the middle, and apartments are the lowest (highest capitalization rate).

Sponsors mark Notes Receivable and Notes Payable to the market according to accounting rules. Essentially the adjustment to market is made when the notes are taken or given according to interest rates prevailing at the time of the transaction. Interest rates change. The balance sheet value of the Notes remains the same. The balance sheet values, while stated as "discounted" (meaning marked to the market), will not necessarily reflect the value at current interest rates.

THE BEST SOLUTION

Finding out where a partnership investment stands is a complicated, laborious task. True, as you use the method outlined in this chapter, you'll become more proficient. But the answer you derive will still be a rough approximation of property performance. The one million investors putting over $12 billion into RELPs each year deserve better reporting.

Real estate sponsors should come out of the dark ages in terms of financial reporting and show financial statements both on a GAAP basis and on a fair market value basis. This additional information, plus adjustments for discontinued operations, give investors an idea of trends in values and an idea of the real worth of investments—a notion long overdue in the real estate limited partnership business.

INDEX

251

252

255